EX LIBRIS

Garden

of the Senses

Garden
of the Senses

*Bringing scent, sound, taste, texture and
visual drama into your garden*

Jenny Hendy

LORENZ BOOKS

Dedication

For my parents who started me on the gardening trail.

This edition is published by Lorenz Books

Lorenz Books is an imprint of Anness Publishing Ltd
Hermes House, 88–89 Blackfriars Road, London SE1 8HA
tel. 020 7401 2077; fax 020 7633 9499
www.lorenzbooks.com
info@anness.com

© 2002 Anness Publishing Ltd

Published in the USA by Lorenz Books, Anness Publishing Inc.
27 West 20th Street, New York, NY 10011; fax 212 807 6813

Published in Australia by Lorenz Books, Anness Publishing Pty Ltd
Level 1, Rugby House, 12 Mount Street, North Sydney, NSW 2060
tel. (02) 8920 8622; fax (02) 8920 8633

This edition distributed in the UK by Aurum Press Ltd
25 Bedford Avenue, London WC1B 3AT
tel. 020 7637 3225; fax 020 7580 2469

This edition distributed in the USA by National Book Network
4720 Boston Way, Lanham, MD 20706
tel. 301 459 3366; fax 301 459 1705; www.nbnbooks.com

This edition distributed in Canada by General Publishing
895 Don Mills Road, 400–402 Park Centre, Toronto, Ontario M3C 1W3
tel. 416 445 3333; fax 416 445 5991; www.genpub.com

This edition distributed in New Zealand by David Bateman Ltd
30 Tarndale Grove, Off Bush Road, Albany, Auckland
tel. (09) 415 7664; fax (09) 415 8892

A CIP catalogue record for this book is available from the British Library.

Publisher Joanna Lorenz
Managing Editor Helen Sudell
Art Manager Clare Reynolds
Project Editor Simona Hill
Designer Louise Clements
Editorial Readers Jonathan Marshall and Richard McGinlay
Production Controller Ann Childers
Text by Jenny Hendy

10 9 8 7 6 5 4 3 2 1

contents

introduction

A garden of the senses is a distillation of the perfect pleasures of the natural world: harmonious colours and elegant shapes, birdsong and breezes, cool grass and heady scents. Creating such a garden begins with letting your senses take over.

When you begin to shape a garden you tend to concentrate on getting the right look, but as nature weaves its spell, the senses come into play, enriching the whole experience. Sit quietly in the open air, tuning into the natural environment that surrounds you, and all the ideas you need to design your perfect space will crystallize. There are many practical things you can do to make a beautiful garden, but you will finally understand all that it has to offer when you appreciate not only what you see, but also all that you hear, taste, touch and smell.

Many people come to gardening when they have their own place or later in life when their children grow up and leave home. Others enjoy creating a garden around their young families. For some people gardening is more a chore than a delight, and there is always hard work to be done, but there are also great rewards, and many small pleasures can be found in the seasonal tasks of turning the soil, sowing and planting, pruning and harvesting.

Gardening can represent a return to a childlike state of wonderment, with freedom to explore and experiment. The effort, enthusiasm and love that can be poured into the garden while nurturing the plants and wildlife is always handsomely repaid. Gardening is a means of self-expression and since we all have different tastes, we produce gardens of infinite variety. The rewards of gardening are many, but perhaps the most important is to create a place where we can easily find tranquillity and peace.

OPPOSITE *The garden is a constant source of inspiration, forever changing with the seasons but also through the day as the light moves round, illuminating different areas.*

THE RESTORATIVE EFFECTS OF A GARDEN

Spending time in the sanctuary of the garden can leave you feeling restored mentally, physically and emotionally. Whatever the stresses and frustrations of your day, if you simply walk out into the garden and take a few deep breaths, absorbing the soothing effect of green foliage and listening to the sounds of nature, you can feel calmer and more contented. Gardens are full of potential for enjoyment, relaxation and contemplation, and they really do have the power to transform negative emotions.

There is something about watching plants grow, develop and change with the seasons that is always uplifting. No matter what else is going on in your world, spring, summer, autumn and winter come and go regardless, and the activities of birds and other creatures continue

ABOVE Summer borders overflow with an abundance of blooms; the air is filled with fragrance and the humming of visiting insects.

in a reassuring and familiar way. And gardens are never static places: even in the depths of winter, when most plants are dormant, the light shifts constantly and the weather is always changing, creating different moods and impressions each day.

THE SENSORY APPROACH

In the process of making a garden that appeals to all the senses, you will almost certainly find that your own sensitivity to sights, sounds, tastes, textures and scents steadily increases. Not only in your own garden, but wherever you go, you will start to feel more strongly integrated with the natural environment, more deeply involved with and affected by everything you experience.

Looking at something beautiful, such as sunlight shining through leaves; hearing the sound of birds singing; smelling the rich aroma of damp earth; tasting a freshly grown herb; or feeling the softness of silken grass heads affects us on an emotional level if we allow ourselves a moment truly to experience and just be. We may feel sadness at the approach of winter, and that emotion could lead us into a quieter, more reflective mood. Equally, the new shoots pushing up through the warming soil in early spring will fill us with elation and hope for the future.

BELOW *This light-hearted border edging reminds us that both fingers and toes can enjoy the garden.*

Before you begin to make changes to an existing garden, or start work on a new plot, give yourself plenty of opportunity to respond to the garden with all your senses. It is more difficult to do this in the middle of winter and you will have to rely largely on memory as you stroll around picturing in your mind's eye the various plants, trees and flowers. Take out a chair so that you can sit for a while in different spots in the garden, and just close your eyes. We usually rely on sight almost completely and to the detriment of our other senses. This overemphasis on sight leads to "looking without seeing", and can suppress our intuitive and creative abilities. Be patient, breathe in the fresh air and let your mind become still. Feel the

After the first impressions have formed in your mind you can create a garden plan in which each of the five senses plays a significant role.

RIGHT *Bright foliage plants, like this* Choisya ternata *'Sundance', stand out among the many darker shades of green.*

OPPOSITE *With the lime-green heads of euphorbia growing through the gaps, this beautiful old window frame is slowly being absorbed into the fabric of the garden. It brings to mind the romantic image of a ruined abbey.*

warmth of the sun's rays or the coolness of the breeze. Listen to the sounds all around you, those close by and more distant. See if you can pick up any scents or fragrances. The longer you sit peacefully observing, the more you will begin to notice.

When you eventually open your eyes, look carefully around, slowly taking in everything you can see. Remember that shadow and darkness are as important as colour and light in shaping the garden picture. Look at what is beyond the garden's boundaries, and ask yourself whether any part of that scene could be incorporated into your overall design. Then draw on all these ideas as you put together your garden plan.

BEGINNING WITH SIGHT

Try to imagine you are looking at the garden through the eyes of an artist. How does the way the light changes through the day affect the appearance of the garden? How do the plants alter in size and colour with the seasons? Don't feel restricted by what is already there, but let your imagination run free. What would be your ideal view? An old-fashioned cottage garden may appeal to a romantic, carefree nature, or perhaps you would prefer to be reminded of summer holidays in hot, dry landscapes, and would enjoy bright Mediterranean-style plantings in terracotta pots. Also think about how colour might be used to enhance different areas of the garden – the sunny spots may be just right for hot reds and oranges, while the slightly cooler places may suit meditative violet and mauve planting schemes. Or perhaps minimalism is more to your taste, with a limited palette, restrained planting and simple architectural shapes.

INCORPORATING SOUND

Most of us dream of a peaceful, quiet oasis where we can relax and escape from the rigours of the day. We may need to muffle unwanted noise from outside the garden, using decorative screens clothed with lush greenery, to achieve this ideal. However, other sounds have a positive effect on the psyche, and one of the most soothing is that of trickling water. No garden is complete without the sounds of birds, insects and wildlife, and most of these visitors also benefit the garden in other ways. The rustle of leaves in the breeze and the gentle tinkling of wind chimes also make wonderful mood-enhancing additions. And if you have children, the sounds of their laughter and play will fill your garden with life.

THE PLEASURES OF TASTE

As you wander through the garden in early summer, what could be more exciting than reaching down to pick a ripe, fragrant strawberry and eating it straight from the plant? Home-grown fruits and vegetables are far fresher and more delicious than anything you can

ABOVE The old-fashioned runner bean variety 'Painted Lady', trained over willow arches, makes a highly ornamental feature.

ABOVE *A wildlife pond is a wonderful place to sit with your eyes closed, just listening. Water attracts all kinds of insects, birds and other creatures, each of which has its own unique call or sound.*

buy. They can also look just as beautiful as ornamental species when they are planted imaginatively. Include jewel-like soft fruits and unusual varieties of apples, pears or plums. A small tree or a few fruit bushes will fit comfortably in the smallest of gardens. Colourful salad leaves, courgettes (zucchini) and ornamental vegetables such as globe artichokes and ruby chard, all make stunning additions. In a tiny garden, make small plantings of vegetables in the flower borders, or grow salad crops and aromatic herbs in pots on the patio.

DESIGNING FOR TOUCH

Many plants invite touch: think of the waxy petals of lilies, or poppies like crumpled silk, ferociously spiked yuccas or the furry leaves of *Stachys lanata*. But the sense of touch is not just about plants: the architectural framework of the garden can include a variety of tactile surfaces. Smooth pebbles and sinuous sculptures contrast with rough-hewn rocks, gravel or slate shards. Remember the appeal of walking barefoot on the beach, and evoke that sense of freedom with areas of sand, pebbles and wooden boardwalks.

THE BEAUTY OF SCENT

Our sense of smell is intimately linked to our emotions and memory, and delicious scents, especially the natural aromas of flowers, leaves and fruits, have a powerful uplifting effect. Incorporating plants with beautiful scents into the garden helps to create a serene and happy atmosphere. Many bulbs, perennials and shrubs have fragrant blooms and even in winter there are a surprising number to choose from. Climbers perfume the air and conveniently provide flowers at nose level, while aromatic herbs crushed underfoot or between the fingers release therapeutic oils. You can even include a few surprises, with plants that have flowers smelling of chocolate or pineapple-scented foliage.

TAKING YOUR TIME

When you are planning to make major changes in the garden, try to avoid being too impulsive and doing everything straight away. What seems the obvious solution to a problem in the spring may give way to a better idea in the autumn, and while you may have a host of different ideas for transforming the garden, it usually takes time for the option that is right for you to rise to the forefront of your consciousness. Certainly, if you have just moved and taken over an established garden, it will take a full year for you to appreciate how all the shrubs, perennials and bulbs perform.

Be very wary about clearing too many of the trees and larger shrubs in an older garden, since these give it a feeling of maturity and continuity. They are also bound to support the garden's wildlife population. By waiting and watching through the seasons, you will come to understand the total environment of your garden.

The garden is not just a picture to look at, but a complex combination of sensual experiences. Just as a composer arranges individual notes to create a beautiful piece of music, the elements of the garden coalesce into a satisfying whole, to which you can respond with all your senses.

OPPOSITE *Old garden tools have a wonderfully mellow feel. If you are lucky you may inherit a collection like this.*

BELOW LEFT *Group pots and containers together to make a colourful focal point that can be moved around the garden.*

sight

Creating a garden teaches us to appreciate natural beauty — the play of light and
shadow, the colours of the flowers and foliage, the changing seasons.

garden pictures

Like an artist applying paint to canvas, we can use all the different visual elements of the garden — colour, shape and texture — to express ourselves in pictures that are constantly developing and changing.

BELOW *Strong contrasting colours — the shades of blue of the doorway and wooden seat and the pink and red geraniums — make a bold statement.*

Our first, and dominant, impression of a garden is of the way it looks, and most ornamental plants are chosen for their visual appeal: either because they have beautiful flowers, leaves or berries, or because they have an elegant or unusual form. The art of garden design lies in creating a series of pictures to enjoy as we move slowly through the garden, and in placing the plants we love to look at in settings that enhance their beauty, so that we can appreciate them individually and in harmony with each other.

Garden pictures need to be composed just like paintings or photographs. Consider how views will be framed, and think about lighting effects, abstract shapes and focal points. We tend to think about the aesthetics of colour, but it can also be used to "shape" a vista. Bright colours such as scarlet and orange catch the eye, and if you want to avoid foreshortening the view, it is best to keep these "advancing" colours in the foreground. Blues, purples and greys, which are the colours of far-off hills in a landscape, are "receding" colours and you can safely use these anywhere, but if you want to create the illusion of distance, place them towards the end of the plot.

The most eye-catching effects are often created by limiting the palette to a few key colours: white is an easy choice, as there are so many plants to choose from. This makes for a coherent look, avoiding sensory overload. The key to success is to mix in a few other shades to enhance the main colour.

OPPOSITE *Gertrude Jekyll was famed for bringing an awareness of colour harmonies to gardening through her knowledge of art. Using the arrangement of colours in the artist's colour wheel, she selected complementary and contrasting shades of flowers and foliage to produce stunning herbaceous borders.*

BELOW LEFT *A carefully trimmed carpet of moss reveals a chequerboard pattern of granite slabs in this Zen-inspired garden. Limiting the palette puts the focus on design.*

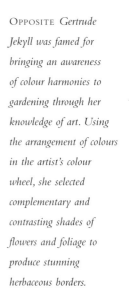

wild at heart

If you live in the middle of the city but your heart is in the countryside, there are many ways in which you can incorporate aspects of the natural landscape into your garden.

BELOW *Spare land can be converted into a wildflower meadow with meandering paths and a scarecrow as a focal point.*

If you feel a strong connection with a wild place such as the seashore or forest, you can include elements of the landscape to evoke its atmosphere in your own garden. If the garden is shaded by mature trees, take advantage of this by creating a woodland glade. Natural woodland has a tiered understorey, so plant shade-tolerant shrubs beneath the trees. Hydrangeas, skimmias and Japanese maples planted with bamboos, herbaceous perennials, carpeting plants and bulbs are ideal. Many woodlanders such as azaleas and rhododendrons, camellias and pieris require neutral to acid soil. You could also plant your own mini-woodland using close-planted saplings of the same or mixed species. Add narrow paths of chipped bark or boardwalks of reclaimed wood.

On a sunny site in poor soil you could create the jewelled look of a wildflower meadow. Sow a wildflower seed mixture in pots, as established plants will take hold better among existing grass, and plant small bulbs to naturalize. Cut the meadow just twice a year, in early spring and late summer.

The garden pond could become the basis of a natural water garden, or you could suggest the presence of water by skilful planting. For example, you could make a stream garden by digging out a shallow trench, lining it with a perforated pond liner and back-filling with good garden soil. Restricting the drainage like this creates the right conditions for leafy bog plants. Add a wooden bridge to complete the picture.

OPPOSITE *A shady corner where the soil never really dries out can be the perfect spot for a bog garden. Log-slice stepping stones add to the waterside feel along with lush plantings of ornamental sedges, rushes, arum lilies and candelabra primulas.*

BELOW LEFT *A boardwalk with shingle or gravel, planted with ornamental grasses, creates a seaside atmosphere.*

feast for the eyes

If you love to grow your own produce, take a fresh look at fruit and vegetables: they can be just as decorative as flowers if you arrange them formally in an elegant potager.

BELOW This opulent kitchen garden has at its centre an elegant birdcage-like structure used to protect ripening fruits. The arrangement of herbs, topiarized fruit trees and vegetables is beautiful to look at.

A potager is a type of ornamental kitchen garden, with ground-level patterns made by arranging the beds within a geometric framework. The design is emphasized by a decorative edging such as terracotta tiles or clipped dwarf box hedging, or less formal edgings of lavender, chives, stepover apples or alpine strawberries. Topiary is another traditional element that helps to give the garden structure, using formal shapes such as spheres, cones, spirals and perhaps some elegant round-headed standards.

Although essentially a productive garden, the emphasis is on aesthetics, so not only the design of the beds but also the choice and arrangement of plants should reflect this. Vegetables, fruits, herbs and flowers are arranged in blocks creating a visual tapestry of shapes, textures and colours. Plants with edible blooms such as nasturtium, pot marigold (*Calendula*), and cottage garden pinks add further splashes of colour. When harvesting leaves gaps, the solution is to use quick-maturing salad crops and hardy annuals as fillers.

Paths of gravel or herringbone brickwork suit the old-fashioned feel, and you can add height by erecting surrounding "walls" of decorative trellis to support fan- or espalier-trained fruit trees. An arched tunnel over a central path could be used to grow beans, squashes, nasturtiums or sweet peas. Wooden obelisks, woven willow cones and rustic wigwams of pea sticks or canes also add height, and have a pleasing profile in winter when the garden is relatively bare.

ABOVE In the potager, pattern and decoration come from the design and layout of pathways as well as from planting. Line routes with decorative fruits and colourful vegetables such as ruby chard, red-leaved lettuce and yellow-fruited courgettes (zucchini) or with herbs such as the lavender (illustrated).

romantic reflections

The carefree atmosphere of a traditional cottage garden is very seductive. Even if you don't live in a cottage, you can enjoy the exuberance and abundance of this old-fashioned style.

RIGHT *An old-fashioned planting of English roses mingled with clematis surrounds this romantic figure of a water carrier. The trellis panel provides a pleasing backdrop as well as creating privacy.*

BELOW RIGHT *Soft grey-green woodwork makes a subtle foil for a pink and purple cottage-style planting of ornamental alliums, bearded iris and lilies. A window box filled with petunias, variegated helichrysum and geraniums creates a focal point.*

The key to success is to superimpose a rampant mixture of plants on a very simple ground plan such as one with straight pathways and rectangular beds. Allow the plants to follow their natural inclinations: the borders should look relaxed, with flowers tumbling out over the paths, sprouting up through cracks in the paving and twining irrepressibly through the larger shrubs. We tend to think of romantic gardens as having only delicate flowers in pastel shades, but a cottage garden can be much more boisterous than this: mix in stronger forms such as globe artichokes or sunflowers, and add vivid splashes of colour to give the planting substance. The aim is to create a garden that looks as if it simply evolved over time, with no particular theme or style, but with lots of pretty flowers tucked into every available space.

For hard landscaping features, concentrate on materials with an "organic" feel that weather easily and well, such as paths of gravel or slate shards edged with wooden gravel boards, country-style fencing such as wicker hurdles or heather panels, and plant supports made from prunings or woven willow. Decorative accessories shouldn't be too ornate. Choose rustic furniture, plain terracotta or stoneware pots and barrels as well as anything that once had a practical use: an old copper kettle or milk churn, a second-hand chair restored with a lick of paint, a beehive or an old-fashioned hand pump.

an image of paradise

The classic design of the cool, tranquil Islamic garden was intended to represent paradise, and in the West, too, gardeners through the ages have tried to recreate a vision of heaven on earth.

BELOW *A winged cherub draws the eye to this little fountain. Symbolic statuary could be important for creating the right atmosphere in your paradise garden.*

CENTRE *The Moorish influence is strongly evident in this English country garden with its formal long axis and rill leading to a temple-like building.*

The Islamic culture produced some of the most exquisite representations of paradise, with shaded courtyards decorated with mosaic tiles, rills feeding into large formal pools, and fountains helping to create a cool, refreshing atmosphere. The symbolic ground plans of both Moorish gardens and Christian monastic gardens had a structured, geometric outline. In monastery gardens the layout was based on the shape of the cross, with a fountain or well at the centre. Within the monastery walls there would also have been a medicinal herb garden. The idea of a tranquil space of quiet retreat is just as attractive today, and we can combine elements of these paradise gardens, filled with aromatic herbs and scented flowers, to create a haven of our own, cutting off the outside world with trellis panels, tall hazel hurdles or formal clipped hedging.

Moisture helps to capture fragrant oils released into the atmosphere, so a central pond and fountain are ideal. A rectangular pool lined with blue mosaic tiles adds a Moorish touch, and you could emphasize the formality of the design by placing a row of identical terracotta pots down each side, perhaps planted with agapanthus.

Herbs like plenty of room to grow and have a tendency to sprawl. Consequently, a geometric layout with wide brick or stone paths will contain them attractively. Incorporate fragrant flowers and consider building a scented arbour to sit under.

BELOW *Imagine what it would be like to stroll through this rose tunnel on a sultry summer's evening, the grassy path scattered with petals and the air heavy with perfume. You could create a similar feature by building a pergola walkway smothered in jasmine or honeysuckle.*

contemplative view

Creating a garden of mystery, with winding paths and hidden corners, allows you to feel as if you have passed into another realm.

ABOVE *Unusual sculptures or natural objects waiting to be discovered enhance your journey through the garden and promote a more contemplative frame of mind.*

As you wander through lush plantings listening to the sound of water, you can be subtly revitalized by drawing on the garden's energy. The background of greenery and soothing flower shades helps you to relax, and, as your mind clears, you become more contemplative, in tune with nature and your own spirituality.

Try to recreate the dappled green light and sense of enclosure of a woodland walk and make a gradual transition from the low light levels indoors to the bright sunshine outside. Consider building a pergola covered in vines and fragrant climbers and set up a bubbling water feature close by. If the plot is very open, you could construct a climber-covered walkway that connects the pergola to a secluded sitting area such as a rustic bower of woven willow covered in honeysuckle or a bench seat by a pool. Plant little copses of saplings and quick-growing shrubs such as laurel, bamboo, *Elaeagnus* x *ebbingei*, variegated and coloured leaf elders and dogwoods for shade and seclusion.

Enhance the "other-worldly" feel by hanging bells and wind chimes wherever they will catch the breeze. Use iridescent glass beads in place of cobbles for water features and make mystical paving patterns using pebbles. Set mirror shards to glint as you pass by and place polished metal orbs that reflect the greenery around them. Sculptures of mythical creatures half-hidden in the undergrowth add a touch of mystery.

BELOW LEFT *This Japanese garden generates an air of tranquillity. The symbolic stream made from pebbles "flows" into the pool and the lantern perches on an island of water lilies.*

BELOW *In a secluded corner, a pagan god wall-mask set into an ivy-clad rock face spouts water into a small mossy pool. The atmosphere is that of an enchanted grotto.*

mediterranean vision

If you have a warm, sunny courtyard, use strong colours, vibrant flowers and masses of aromatic herbs in terracotta pots to create an outdoor room inspired by the easy-going Mediterranean summer lifestyle.

There is nothing rigid or formal about Mediterrean style. It is all about letting go, and it creates the perfect environment for winding down at the end of the day.

For the floor of your outdoor room, choose gravel, cobbles, stone-effect paving or slate tiles. Rendered, painted walls continue the theme. Ordinary brick walls can be camouflaged with trellis panels painted in soft powder blue, or bamboo fence roll. A pergola could provide support for a grapevine or wisteria that will cast dappled shade. Furniture could be built-in bench seating or simple café-style tables and chairs with plenty of colourful cushions. Outdoor lighting is essential: hang up candle lanterns or switch on tiny white fairy lights. A large urn or oil jar makes a strong statement, and a wall fountain trickling into a raised pool will create a wonderfully evocative atmosphere.

Simple terracotta pots and wall planters, or rough peasant pottery, are perfect for vibrantly coloured plants. If you have somewhere to overwinter tender plants, there are a host of suitable subtropical specimens – potted figs, citrus plants, angel's trumpets (*Brugmansia suaveolens*), cannas and even the deliciously fragrant ginger lilies (*Hedychium*). Plants that can be enjoyed in the cool of the evening include the fragrant four o'clock plant (*Mirabilis jalapa*), jasmine and honeysuckle. For a truly Mediterranean feel, include herbs like thyme, rosemary and oregano and, of course, vivid pelargoniums and drought-tolerant succulents like agave, echeveria and houseleeks (*Sempervivum*).

pattern and repetition

Even when very little colour is included, an architectural garden design can be visually exciting, emphasizing the importance of form and texture, light and shade.

BELOW *An avenue of conifers will have a wonderfully strong profile in winter. A pergola could produce the same kind of rhythm along a pathway.*

When you are planning a formal garden it helps to visualize the scene in black and white to bring out its structural elements. If you are trying to improve an existing garden, you can take a series of black-and-white photographs to show you where the strength of your design lies and which areas lack substance.

The framework of the garden is most apparent in winter, when its structure is exposed. Topiary or a clipped evergreen hedge that was largely camouflaged by foreground planting in summer assumes greater significance in the quiet season. Even with very loose, informal planting, you need a strong ground plan to hold the design together and solid architectural or sculptural features to provide contrast and visual interest. These elements might range from statuesque or bold-leaved specimen plants to a large glazed pot or wrought-iron seat. Enhance architectural and sculptural elements and make bold foliage plants such as yucca and phormium even more dramatic with the aid of mini spotlights positioned to shine from below or from the side.

When you introduce some kind of visual repetition in the garden, the eye is instantly drawn to it. Setting up a rhythm can be very pleasing and restful, but straight

ABOVE *The curious pattern of hub-caps set into this broad gravel path really excites the imagination. Further along, the path passes beneath an unusual arch made from birch branches.*

OPPOSITE *Carved stone spheres set at an equal distance from one another generate a surreal but restful atmosphere. You could achieve a similar effect with topiary shapes.*

lines tend to work better in a garden of formal design. Here you might place glazed ceramic balls or topiary cones at regular intervals to mark the edge of a path, and the pattern made by fencing posts can be emphasized by topping each one with an acorn or ball-shaped finial. In an informal setting, consider setting out shapes in a spiral, arc or circle.

Smooth, flat, open spaces such as lawns, paving or decking, which contrast with riotous borders, are restful to the eye, and formal ground patterns sculpted from low clipped hedging including box, lavender and santolina can also be very pleasing. Make a parterre or knot garden, or create a simple chequerboard design.

hot and dazzling

Reds and oranges are the visual pick-me-up of the garden world. They vitalize and stimulate us, fill us with energy and passion, and lift our spirits.

ABOVE LEFT *Spring, summer and autumn bulbs can be used to inject colour into existing plantings, strengthening schemes and introducing dramatic seasonal changes.*

Many people who live in cool climates are attracted to hot colours but find them difficult to incorporate. Although bright tones are often used in contemporary settings they are considered quite daring. It is possibly because they are so vibrant and attention-grabbing that people tend to be nervous of using them. Glowing cerise, scarlet, flame orange and magenta create strong focal points whenever they appear in the garden.

In a plot large enough to be divided into compartments you can afford to be quite theatrical with these dazzling shades, turning one whole garden room into a tropical

ABOVE RIGHT *Just when the summer border is beginning to fade, dahlias burst into flower with all the sizzling reds, oranges and clashing pinks you could want.*

extravaganza. For an exotic touch try canna, large-flowered cactus, dahlias, alstroemerias, trumpet lilies, *Geranium psilostemon*, daylilies, red hot pokers and crocosmia, and mix in plenty of rich green foliage plants. Many of the annuals and tender perennials also offer intense tones, including fuchsia, verbena, petunia, busy Lizzie, geranium and nasturtium. Use them to put zing into containers and baskets. Annual rudbeckias such as the rich golden 'Marmalade' are useful for adding punch to bright borders. For foreground planting around subtropical-looking specimens try patio plants such as the vivid new verbena varieties, gazanias and cerise or magenta osteospermums.

If you want to create a display suggesting intense heat, use bronze and maroon foliage plants like bronze fennel, purple-leaved *Cotinus coggygria* and *Berberis* x *ottawensis* f. *purpurea*, *Physocarpus opulifolius* 'Diabolo', bronze-leaved cannas and the dark heucheras such as *H.* 'Palace Purple' as a foil for scarlet and burnt-orange blooms.

Hot displays are easier to create towards the end of the summer and into autumn when oranges and reds predominate in flowers and fruit. In spring use tulips, wallflowers and cerise aubrieta in sunny spots, and for shady areas try rhododendrons, pieris, camellias and brilliantly coloured deciduous azaleas.

tranquil and relaxing

Purple and violet have long been associated with the sacred, with mysticism and higher thought.
Exposure to these colours is said to calm, relax and inspire us, and to promote spirituality.

If you want to create a calming garden environment conducive to freeing the mind of everyday matters, then soft blues and purples should predominate.

Although there are eye-catching shades of blue and purple these are usually gentle colours, lacking impact. When they are used exclusively they can create a moody and subdued atmosphere in the garden. To avoid dullness, mix in some velvety crimson, burgundy, magenta and cerise blooms; bronze, maroon, silver and metallic foliage; and scatterings of white flowers. Alternatively, create a focal point with a piece of sculpture or a fountain.

In a place designed for meditation, bright sunlight can be intrusive, so it helps to create dappled shade using trees and shrubs or a pergola covered with blue and purple climbers such as wisteria, clematis or potato vine (*Solanum crispum* 'Glasnevin'). In the area below, plant shade-tolerant shrubs such as hydrangeas (neutral to acid soil is required for blue or purple flowers), rhododendrons, *Leycesteria formosa*, Japanese maples and hardy fuchsias. There

FAR LEFT *Purple verbenas and ivy-leafed geraniums make a subtle combination for a hanging basket.*

BELOW *Cool blues, mauve-pinks and purples are lifted by touches of white and silver foliage and flowers and polished steel containers planted with white-barked birch trees. The scheme would be more restful with a plain, deep green backdrop.*

BELOW LEFT *Soft purples and lilac-blues suit the serene atmosphere of a meditation garden. If you want to compose your thoughts and relax, spend some time sitting amongst these calming shades.*

is more choice with perennials, beginning in spring with *Brunnera macrophylla, Helleborus hybridus* cultivars, *Symphytum* 'Hidcote Blue', dicentras, pulmonarias and violas; moving into summer with drumstick alliums, *Lilium martagon,* aquilegias, herbaceous geraniums, Himalayan poppies, astrantias, *Campanula latifolia*, hostas and monkshoods (*Aconitum*). *Phlox paniculata* does surprisingly well in dappled shade in late summer, and in autumn the curious toad lilies appear. For bulbs choose from camassias, bluebells, grape hyacinths, scillas and autumn-flowering crocus and colchicums.

A herb garden is a favourite place for contemplation. Most herbs possess purple-tinted blooms, including thyme, lavender, rosemary, mint, marjoram, sage, clary sage and hyssop. Augment these plants with sun-loving, drought-tolerant aromatic perennials and shrubs including Russian sage (*Perovskia atriplicifolia* 'Blue Spire'), catmint, *Caryopteris* x *clandonensis* 'Heavenly Blue' and *Cistus* x *purpureus*, and add perfume with buddleia, lilac and old-fashioned roses such as *Rosa* 'William Lobb' and *R.* 'Cardinal de Richelieu'.

In the sunny mixed border try the deciduous *Ceanothus* x *delileanus* 'Gloire de Versailles' with its powder blue "puffs", and for autumn use late-flowering hebes and penstemons, such as *P.* 'Blackbird', *Hibiscus syriacus* 'Oiseau Bleu' and *Ceratostigma willmottianum*. In winter and spring varieties of heathers *Erica carnea* and *E.* x *darleyensis* come to the fore.

ABOVE *Glass beads in graduated shades of blue have been used to line this water feature, creating a watery whirlpool design.*

soft and gentle

Delicate pastel shades are restful to the eye. They are the colours of the romantic garden and help to create the effect of a safe haven with a soothing, comforting atmosphere.

Pink is a key colour in the pastel palette. It symbolizes love, and in colour therapy is believed to have profound healing qualities. Pink varies from the yellow-pinks, like salmon and apricot, to the blue-pinks, such as glowing lilac, and at the most vivid extreme, cerise. The many shades of green in the garden make a wonderful foil for pink flowers. Silver, grey and glaucous leaves all work well with blue-pinks, while lime and apple-green foliage and flowers and yellow-variegated leaves form an excellent partnership with yellow-pinks and clear pinks. Virtually all pink flowers will blend together, so if you want a feminine, all-pink border, include everything from deep to very pale pink, and mix flower forms for maximum contrast. Add more substantial foliage plants, such as the pink and white variegated *Acer negundo* 'Flamingo', cardoons (like giant silver thistles) and blue-leaved hostas, to keep the border from looking ill-defined and amorphous.

The rose is the quintessential flower of the romantic garden, and its flower shape contrasts beautifully with traditional herbaceous perennials such as lady's mantle, campanulas, sidalceas, herbaceous geraniums, catmints and artemisias. There are forms of rose to suit all locations, from low ground-cover types such as *Rosa* 'Flower Carpet', to neat bushes like *R.* 'Gentle Touch' for growing at the front of the border or around a patio. Then there are the old-fashioned English roses including *R.* 'Heritage' and 'Mary Rose' with sumptuous blooms, and shrub roses for the back of the border such as *R.* 'Marguerite Hilling'. Beautiful climbers include *R.* 'New Dawn' and the apricot-tinged 'Compassion'. Choose disease-resistant and repeat-flowering cultivars to cut down on maintenance and provide you with an attractive and consistent display.

Another flower that seems to have been created for lovers is the peony, a lovely example being *Paeonia* 'Sarah Bernhardt', with fragrant, double, apple-blossom pink blooms. Combine it with the diaphanous blue annual, love-in-a-mist (*Nigella*), and the sculpted flowers of the soft blue *Iris pallida* subsp. *pallida*.

Some flowers soften and fade as they age, taking on an even more romantic appearance. The papery heads of hydrangeas undergo such a metamorphosis, echoing the colours of faded silks and tapestries. Sometimes the pale pink or white petals become suffused with other colours such as jade green, or are mottled with raspberry. The lovely white-flowered *Hydrangea* 'Madame Emile Mouillère', together with several of the white *H. paniculata* cultivars, are charmingly blushed with pink.

sunny and stimulating

Yellow energizes, bringing vitality and vibrancy to lift a dull flower border. The eye notices yellow immediately, so even an odd scattering can have a big effect.

The yellow flowers of early spring – aconites, daffodils and crocus – have a wonderfully cheering effect after the dark winter, and throughout the year yellow flowers light up the garden, even on the dullest days.

From cream to pale lemon, primrose and butter yellow, deepening to pure chrome yellow or gold, you can find flowers to blend into any scheme. Yellow daisies with a tinge of orange prevail in late summer, and in the golden light, with a backdrop of turning leaves and ripening berries, flowers such as *Rudbeckia* 'Herbstsonne' and

'Goldsturm', helianthus and heliopsis really seem to glow. Lemon and acid yellow, with a higher proportion of green, look stunning with vivid purples, cerise and magenta. Try the yellow trumpets of *Hemerocallis* 'Marion Vaughn' with *Geranium psilostemon*. Blue is also an excellent partner for yellow: the gentler blues with a hint of purple such as many of the campanulas, herbaceous geraniums and *Aster* x *frikartii* 'Mönch' look good with creamy yellows like *Anthemis tinctoria* 'Sauce Hollandaise', *Coreopsis verticillata* 'Moonbeam', *Kniphofia* 'Little Maid' and *Phygelius aequalis* 'Yellow Trumpet'.

An all-yellow planting can work well in a shady area, giving the effect of a pool of sunlight in a forest clearing. Not all yellow flowers are happy in shade but some yellow-leaved foliage plants will tolerate it. Try the yellow-variegated dogwood, *Cornus alba* 'Spaethii', hostas such as *H.* 'Sum and Substance' and 'Gold Standard', golden creeping Jenny (*Lysimachia nummularia* 'Aurea') and grasses and creeping bamboos including *Milium effusum* 'Aureum', *Hakonechloa macra* 'Aureola' and *Pleioblastus auricomus*. In a semi-wild part of the garden you could use the self-seeding Welsh poppy (*Meconopsis cambrica*) and the dainty fern-leaved *Corydalis lutea*. For good moisture-retentive soil in sun or dappled shade, the 1.8m/6ft spires of *Ligularia* 'The Rocket' live up to their name.

cool and refreshing

In an elegant garden that relies on architectural shapes – green lawns, clipped hedges and formal pools –
a restrained planting of white blooms is all that is necessary to complete the picture.

ABOVE *This tiny balcony garden is a haven of tranquillity because the palette has been limited to cool, calm colours – soft grey treillage, grey-blue juniper topiary, white walls, white hydrangeas and busy Lizzies, and the natural shades of terracotta pots, wooden deck and wicker screen.*

White symbolizes purity and simplicity, and white blooms have a perfect, unmatched beauty. They stand out in the last of the evening light, and are indispensable for planting evocative twilight or moon gardens. You can create a peaceful atmosphere in a garden simply by confining planting to mainly evergreen shrubs and deciduous specimens with subtle foliage effects, highlighting them with a few white and pale green flowers.

To add interest to a white scheme, include every shade of green, such as fizzy lime and apple-green flowers, as well as golden and white- or yellow-variegated foliage. In full sun, silver, grey and steely blue-leaved plants make a significant contribution. With such a restrained planting scheme, white woodwork, pale grey stonework and paving, or hi-tech elements like stainless steel, chrome and clear glass bricks blend beautifully.

White flowers can establish a look of refined elegance. Set a pair of stone- or lead-effect vases on each side of a doorway and plant them with white, lime green and silver annuals and tender perennials. If the entrance is on the shady side of the house, use white busy Lizzies, fuchsias, white-variegated spider plants (*Chlorophytum comosum*) and ivy trails, or for permanent container plantings consider a duo of white mop-head hydrangeas or white-variegated hostas. To give a sunny terrace the flavour of the Riviera, grow scented, white-flowered climbers such as jasmine and *Trachelospermum asiaticum* up the walls, and fill ornate terracotta planters with exotic-looking specimens such as white-flowered oleander, angel's trumpets (*Brugmansia suaveolens*), silver spear (*Astelia chathamica*), the giant tobacco (*Nicotiana sylvestris*) and white-variegated Japanese pittosporum. Cool down the area around a pool or fountain with water colours – mix white flowers with silver and lime green foliage and combine with true blue flowers like *Ceanothus* 'Puget Blue', forget-me-nots, dazzling blue delphiniums and the royal blue *Anchusa azurea* 'Loddon Royalist'.

The great white cherry, *Prunus* 'Taihaku', is a breathtaking sight in full bloom. On a smaller scale there is the ravishing double white lilac (*Syringa vulgaris* 'Madame Lemoine') and frothy hydrangea cultivars such as *Hydrangea paniculata* 'Grandiflora'. Shrubs and climbers with a festooning habit also look superb. You might use one of the white or cream-flowered rambler roses such as *Rosa* 'Sander's White Rambler' or the extremely vigorous *R*. 'Rambling Rector' which can sometimes be seen with its long tresses falling from the branches of a tree. Some of the larger mock oranges like *Philadelphus* 'Beauclerk', which has maroon-blotched white flowers, also produce a cascade effect.

OPPOSITE *Away from the heat of a summer's day, this shady walkway will soothe frayed nerves. Green predominates and touches of white add a refreshing note of elegance and purity. If you want to display sculpture effectively, keep the backdrop simple.*

the outdoor room

During the long, balmy days of summer, no one feels like going indoors when the sun goes down. Make the most of your outdoor living space with magical lighting effects that transform the garden.

BELOW *A dining area set beneath the shade of a large parasol, enveloped by the fragrances and aromas of the garden, generates a relaxed atmosphere that can transform the simplest of meals.*

Eating and drinking *al fresco* can become a truly sensual experience, even when it's just a simple picnic on the lawn or barbecue with friends. Not only does the food taste better, but there is an atmosphere of fun and relaxation. If you do not already have an outdoor dining area, take a look around the garden and see what would make the ideal location – perhaps a spot that catches the morning sunshine so that you can enjoy breakfast there at weekends. When the walls of the house and paving have been warmed by the sun for most of the afternoon, the accumulated heat is radiated back into the air at night. Protected from wind this makes it possible to sit out in comfort well after sundown. A gas-powered patio heater or a rustic chiminea will help to keep you warm on cooler evenings. If you want to create a really special atmosphere, forget about conventional barbecues and get in touch with your primitive ancestry by building a circular fire pit. You can sit around this after dark, mesmerized by the flames, or use them to cook over.

The comfort of your outdoor room deserves special attention. Having some permanent outdoor seating, such as a small hardwood table and chair set or a rustic picnic table with built-in bench seats, will encourage you to sit out whenever it's warm.

Outdoor lighting extends the use of the garden and allows you to create different moods and effects. Consider safety first though, ensuring that steps and changes in level are well lit and illuminating garden paths and the edges of borders with soft, ground-level lighting. Mini floodlights can be quite dramatic when shining up into the branches of a tree, or down on to a small courtyard, and are less harsh than you might expect. Subtle mini-spot uplighters and downlighters are used to pick out points of interest around the garden such as a piece of sculpture, a wall fountain, or an architectural plant like New Zealand flax (*Phormium*). Tiny white fairy lights can be woven through climbers covering a pergola producing the effect of twinkling stars, and candlelight of any kind is always romantic. Enhance the atmosphere of an outdoor dining room with wall-mounted candle sconces and wrought iron candelabras. And for a touch of magic, try candles and lanterns around a still, reflecting pool.

OPPOSITE *Candlelight has a magical effect on the garden, turning an ordinary plot into a wonderland of flickering light and colour.*
TOP LEFT *Make your own candleholders from tin foil plates shaped like flowers, or,* TOP RIGHT, *from recycled glass containers and jam jars.*
BOTTOM *Lanterns come in a wide range of designs and can be fun to mix and match.*

heralds of spring

There is something new to be seen every day in the garden, and the constant process of transformation is at its most exciting when the new buds are swelling and opening in springtime.

BELOW *The cyclamineus daffodils, such as the variety 'Jack Snipe' pictured below, are some of the earliest to flower. Though they look quite dainty and fragile, they are tremendously weather resistant and good for naturalizing or growing beneath deciduous shrubs. Another advantage of these small species is that their foliage dies down unobtrusively.*

Birds and other animals are much more attuned to the seasons than we are, and by watching their activities we often get the first clues that spring is about to arrive. In colder climates, melting snow marks its advent, but in more temperate regions the transformation is no less exciting. Buds begin to swell, shoots appear out of the bare earth and bulbs bloom along with early blossom trees like the ornamental apricot (*Prunus mume* 'Beni-shidori').

As the season progresses, bright, fresh green becomes the overriding colour. The newly emerged leaves of trees and shrubs unfold and expand, and herbaceous foliage seems to burst forth and grow with amazing speed, smothering the ground. One of the most attractive plants to push up early shoots is the daylily with its clumps of striking apple-green leaves. The peony is also noted for the beauty of its emerging stems which are often shaded deep glossy red or purple.

Ducking in and out of rain showers we set to work clearing the debris from the previous season to make way for up-and-coming displays. As the ground dries out and warms up, seeds are sown and new plants set in position. The garden becomes a hive of activity, not just human but also animal, bird and insect. On warm, sunny days it might feel almost like summer, until a sudden cold snap reminds us that we still have a way to go.

Many spring-flowering plants are natives of deciduous woodland. In their natural setting they bloom before the trees come into leaf, while the woodland floor is in dappled sunlight, and some of the most effective spring plantings in the garden are those that capture the informal atmosphere of woodland. Spring is the season of the bulb and there are myriad shades, though yellow, clear blue and white prevail. Plant low-growing weather-resistant types in drifts beneath a specimen tree such as the elegantly sculpted *Magnolia* x *soulangeana*. Try snowdrops, *Iris reticulata*, wood anemones, *Crocus chrysanthus* and *C. tommasinianus* varieties, *Scilla mischtschenkoana* and early daffodils such as *Narcissus* 'Tête-à-Tête'. The large-flowered hyacinths and tulips that bloom slightly later fare best in a sunny border but you can naturalize Dutch crocus and daffodils in grass.

Early perennials are mostly shade tolerant and include drumstick primulas, silver-spotted pulmonarias, fern-leaved dicentras, the yellow daisy flowered doronicums and the bright lime-green grass, *Milium effusum* 'Aureum'. Honesty and forget-me-not seed themselves generously.

ABOVE *Like so many of the early blooms, crocuses seem too fragile for the time of year, and the sight of drifts of crocuses flowering in a lawn is certainly uplifting. These little* Crocus chrysanthus *emerge with the snowdrops.*

OPPOSITE Magnolia x soulangeana *flowers in the middle of spring, at a time when many species of bulbs and herbaceous plants are in flower. You can grow it in a mixed border but it is an even better lawn specimen, especially if you plant a carpet of grape hyacinths (*Muscari*) beneath.*

the bounty of summer

By early summer the garden is festooned with blossom, the luxuriant growth fuelled by warmer nights and frequent showers.

Summer is the time when flowering perennials put on a fabulous show. Some of the most spectacular plants bloom from early to midsummer, including the bearded iris, which come in clear strong colours as well as gorgeous watercolour shades. Statuesque delphinium, lupin, campanula and foxglove spires make a strong contrast with the voluptuous rounded blooms of peonies and old-fashioned roses, or the "frothy" flowers that are a good foil for any plant of substance – silvery artemisias, herbaceous geraniums such as G. 'Johnson's Blue', catmint (*Nepeta* x *faassenii*) and lady's mantle (*Alchemilla mollis*).

Walls and fences disappear beneath abundant flowers and foliage. Climbing partnerships, such as large-flowered clematis twining through climbing roses, can be enchanting, and the tapering racemes of wisteria and *Laburnum* x *watereri* 'Vossii' or the tiered blossoms of *Viburnum plicatum* 'Mariesii' bring a look of opulence to the garden.

Pot plants can be brought out to spend summer on the terrace, and with containers overflowing with brilliant annuals and tender perennials, the garden starts to feel distinctly subtropical. Pots of large-flowered trumpet lilies fit in nicely, as do succulents and spiky architectural plants like agave, yucca, cordyline and phormium.

The giant leaves of moisture-loving plants such as *Rheum palmatum* 'Atrosanguineum', rodgersias and hostas conjure up images of steamy jungle vegetation and a well planted pool can become the centre of attention, acting like a cooling oasis and attracting spectacular insect life, such as dragonflies and damselflies.

BELOW *Elegant cast-iron furniture, potted geraniums and cascading mock orange blooms combine to produce an atmosphere of informality.*

winter's frosty dawn

*We tend to view winter's approach with a degree of sadness, missing the colour and outdoor
living of summer. But winter has its own magical beauty.*

ABOVE LEFT *In winter,
the faded leaves and
flower-heads of herbaceous
plants and grasses
are transformed by hoar
frost into objects of
great beauty.*

For gardeners whose greatest pleasure and satisfaction is in beavering away in the borders,
there is frustration at not being able to work during the winter. However, this is the time
when we can learn to appreciate the tranquillity of the sleeping landscape.

Depending on the climate and prevailing weather, winter has many faces. Sometimes
autumn seems to go on for months with bright sunny days alternating with mists and fog,
and the first bitterly cold night catches us unawares. In other regions, winter appears
almost overnight with the arrival of snow.

ABOVE RIGHT *Red
cotoneaster berries gleam
like jewels in the snow.
On a larger scale, frost
and snow reveal the
architectural form of
the garden.*

During winter, views of the garden assume greater significance. It might be too cold to spend any length of time outdoors but the structure of the garden becomes clearly visible. At times the scene is almost monochrome, with bare branches silhouetted against the sky, dark domes of evergreen shrubs and the clean lines of clipped hedges.

To truly appreciate the winter garden, it must be viewed at close quarters. You'll discover clusters of berries glistening in the sunlight, frosted leaves, stems and seed-heads and occasionally a single bloom whose appearance seems miraculous. Of course you could create a whole border devoted to winter interest. Many winter-flowering plants are so tough that even if the frost kills all the open flowers or the snow smothers them, they continue their display at the first mild spell. Consider red-stemmed dogwoods, for example *Cornus alba* 'Sibirica', or the white-stemmed *Rubus thibetanus*; brightly variegated evergreens such as *Elaeagnus pungens* 'Maculata' and the holly *Ilex altaclarensis* 'Golden King'; colourful conifers and flowering shrubs including *Viburnum* x *bodnantense* 'Dawn', *Mahonia* x *media* 'Winter Sun' and *Daphne bholua* 'Jacqueline Postill'. For foreground planting and ground cover use hellebores, elephant's ears (*Bergenia*) and variegated ivy, and plant clumps of snowdrops, early flowering crocus, scillas and dwarf daffodils.

sound

Close your eyes and listen to the sounds of the garden — wind, water, the wild birds and insects and the rustle of leaves. With them come peace and serenity.

the sound of nature

Few of us ever experience true quietness, and total silence can be unnerving. The "quietness" of the garden is really a tapestry of gentle, natural sounds, lulling us into peace and relaxation.

Natural sounds, such as birdsong or the wind in the trees, are an important element in our enjoyment of the garden. Yet it sometimes takes a while to "tune in" to the wealth of natural melodies that surround us, because we are so used to blocking out the intrusive pitch and volume of the man-made noises that beset us in our everyday lives. Unravelling the multitudinous threads of sound in the garden is a calming exercise. If you close your eyes and listen intently, you can begin to map out your surroundings and create a sound picture. On a warm day you might hear buzzing insects bustling around a shrub in bloom; the flutter of wings close to the bird feeder; wind chimes tinkling, or water cascading. As a breeze stirs the plants, leaves and grasses rustle and you might even catch the small explosion of a ripe seed pod.

The sounds of nature change during the course of the day, and night is an especially evocative time as the birds go to roost and a hushed stillness descends. Under cover of darkness you might hear owls or foxes calling; the high-pitched chattering of tiny mammals as they scurry through the undergrowth; frogs croaking around the pond, or in warmer climes, insects like cicadas. Of course things are not always rosy: you might live next to a main road or noisy neighbours. Fortunately there is much that can be done with planting around the boundaries to muffle unwanted noise.

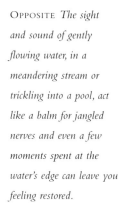

OPPOSITE *The sight and sound of gently flowing water, in a meandering stream or trickling into a pool, act like a balm for jangled nerves and even a few moments spent at the water's edge can leave you feeling restored.*

BELOW LEFT *If your garden is beset by the noises of the busy world outside, concentrate on creating an atmosphere of calm. Cool greens, dappled shade and a feeling of enclosure help you forget the surrounding hubbub. Here, the open space of the octagonal lawn is a void that creates a still centre. The same effect could be achieved with an expanse of gravel or a dark reflecting pool.*

the dawn chorus

Gardens are an important habitat for many species of songbird: encourage them into your plot and they will reward you with their melodious calls from dawn to dusk.

As the sun rises birds begin to announce their presence with liquid warblings and strident declarations of territory. From early spring, right through the breeding season, the air is filled with their musical offerings, and towards the end of the day, as the light begins to fade, you will often hear one or two birds signing off for the night from a safe vantage point. You might not always be able to see which bird is singing – they are often too well camouflaged – but persevere and you may be surprised to discover a tiny creature producing sound of incredible intensity.

At first birdsong seems to be a random jumble of melodies and call-signs but with a bit of detective work you can begin to unravel the different threads and match song to bird. As you become familiar with their tunes, your awareness of the presence of less common visitors will grow. Some birds will just be passing through – *en route* to their winter residence perhaps – and you may be alerted to their presence by an unusual call.

One of the main ways to encourage birds to alight in your garden is to plant trees. They provide a safe perch away from predators, and without them birds will tend to fly across without stopping. Provision of safe drinking and bathing facilities is another big draw. Place birdbaths around the garden, keeping them topped up with fresh water as part of your daily routine, or provide access to a shallow pool. In a wildlife pond you could create a gently shelving beach of cobbles or a ramp of untreated wood. Alternatively, place a large, semi-submerged stone in the water. Birds will also relish a shower created by water splashing down from a cascade or mini-waterfall and will jostle for a turn on a hot, sunny day. Keep the space surrounding drinking, bathing and feeding areas quite open so that there is no cover where predators can lurk unseen.

Providing bird feeders right through the year massively increases bird activity and this is a perfect way to bring them close to the house and outdoor sitting area. The air becomes alive with tweeting and fluttering, and many more species than usual

ABOVE Set bird baths and drinking bowls around the garden and make a point of keeping the water clean and regularly topped up.

BELOW RIGHT Hang a variety of foodstuffs out for the birds, especially during the winter months and don't forget to cater for ground feeding species.

ABOVE *Some birds are particularly sensitive to the use of chemicals, and slug bait can be especially harmful as the birds may unwittingly eat poisoned slugs and snails. It may seem like a drop in the ocean in conservation terms, but it is worth avoiding the use of pesticides where possible, to help protect species like this song thrush.*

are attracted in from surrounding areas. It is surprising how quickly the birds get used to your presence and how bold they become.

Birds will also forage for natural foodstuffs such as insects and caterpillars, keeping the pest population under control, and any soil disturbance will attract species searching for grubs and worms. Keep the use of garden chemicals to a minimum to ensure a plentiful supply of insects for food. Plant shrubs and trees with red or orange fruits and berries and leave at least some seed-heads to develop. At the end of the season, resist the temptation to have a big tidy-up, leaving most of your pruning to the spring. Birds will appreciate the extra cover and food supply as the weather turns cold.

The observation of sound is just one of the many ways in which you can become more attuned to your garden and to nature. You come to realize that this is not just a back yard where plants are grown for pleasure, but a thriving natural habitat supporting an amazing diversity of creatures.

BELOW *Carefully positioned nest boxes may tempt birds but the dense cover of shrubbery or hedging will have as much appeal.*

a steady hum

The low background buzz of bees, hoverflies and other insects idling around the flower borders foraging for nectar and pollen, lasts from spring to autumn.

ABOVE *Give up on chemicals, go organic and let the garden achieve its own equilibrium between pest and predator: you will be creating the perfect home for wildlife.*

If you sit or lie in the garden on a warm summer's day and close your eyes, the constant humming of the busy insects around you can send you into a state of deep relaxation. Apart from the restful sounds they make, insects such as bees, hoverflies and ladybirds are beneficial visitors, pollinating your plants and eating pests such as greenfly. However beautiful your flower border, the presence of buzzing insects complete the picture by making it come alive with sound and movement, so include plants that they like to visit.

Insect attractors include annuals and herbaceous plants such as *Limnanthes douglasii* (poached egg plant), wallflowers, pot marigolds (*Calendula*), sunflowers, white alyssum, *Monarda* (bee balm), herbaceous geraniums, rudbeckias and *Sedum spectabile* (ice plant). Good climbers to add would be fragrant honeysuckles and single-flowered rambling roses. For shrubs, as well as the aptly named butterfly bush (*Buddleja*), try mock orange (*Philadelphus*), hypericums and *Choisya ternata*. Hoverflies favour daisy flowers and single, flat-topped blooms so be sure to include these.

One of the first insect sounds you will hear in spring is the drone of the bumble bee. They particularly like grape hyacinths, though bees will visit all kinds of blooms. On a hot summer's day, in an area where the grass has been allowed to grow long, you may hear crickets and grasshoppers and in warmer climes, at night, the evocative call of cicadas and tree frogs. Where there is a lot of insect activity with water close by, there are sure to be dragonflies and damselflies. These skilful fliers, looking like brilliantly-coloured helicopters, cause a flurry of excitement as they zoom about.

Making a wildlife pond is a great way to attract all kinds of non-human visitors – as well as many different insect species, the water will attract birds, amphibians and mammals, including bats. You can include a small cascade or a fountain, but even without moving water, ponds are never still or quiet. There is the buzz of insects hovering over the surface, the splashing and fluttering of bathing birds and the croaking of frogs. Landscape the pool with a proportion of native plantings and develop a more relaxed approach throughout the garden, turning a blind eye to pockets of weeds and tracts of long grass, and nature will thrive. Undisturbed log, leaf and rock piles will create useful habitats and winter hibernation sites for many creatures.

OPPOSITE *The prominent centre of a coneflower makes an ideal platform for a visiting bee. Experience the sound of bees at close quarters by lying on a lawn of flowering clover or doze off to the humming that emanates from carpeting thymes, lavender and catmint. Most herbs, fragrant flowers and species plants are rich in nectar and therefore good for bees – you can easily detect the honey-sweetness of buddleia, heliotrope and white alyssum in the scent of the flowers.*

rustling leaves

*Air is seldom completely still. The subtlest eddies cause a leaf or flower to flutter or tremble,
and as the wind blows through the plants its energy is translated into sound.*

BELOW *For pleasing
sounds in the autumn
and winter garden allow
the stems of ornamental
grasses and the stiff,
papery seed heads of
shrubs and flowers
to remain.*

Some plants are particularly useful for introducing distinctive sounds into the garden.
Many broad-leaved grasses make a pleasing papery rustling as the blades rub against
each other. If you plant them in large swathes, the breeze causes wave upon wave of
whispering as it passes through them. If you close your eyes it can sometimes sound
like the sea. Try *Miscanthus sinensis* cultivars, pampas, deschampsias, stipas and the fluffy-
flowered pennisetums. Rushes and reeds at the water's edge also make music. Bamboos,
particularly the elegant *Phyllostachys* and *Fargesia* species and cultivars, have long been
noted for their soothing wind songs, and bamboo makes an ideal planting for creating
privacy and seclusion around a sitting area.

Autumn is known for its changeable moods and blustery weather, so make the most
of the sharp gusts that blow up at this time of year by leaving hydrangea
flower-heads and the dried stems and rattle-like seed-heads of
herbaceous plants uncut until the spring.

ABOVE *The sound of
trees in the wind can be
quite mournful, sending
you into a more reflective
mood. It can also be
uplifting and energizing.*

OPPOSITE *It is
mesmerizing to watch
the way the wind causes
wave-like undulations in
the flexible branches of
large bamboo stands.
But even more magical
is the whispering sound
made by the leaves
rubbing together.*

There are particular trees that are well known for the pleasing noise
they make in the wind. With a relatively large garden you might consider
creating a small copse of close-planted trees such as silver birch, to
maximize the sound generated. The aspen (*Populus tremula*) is an American
favourite but other poplars with their fluttering foliage also make good
wind song. The weeping willow of riverbanks comes alive in the breeze.
Be wary of poplars and willows in a garden setting though. The majority
are extremely vigorous, with invasive roots, and should never be sited close
to buildings as they can absorb enough moisture to cause subsidence.

The Scots pine (*Pinus sylvestris*) and Corsican pine (*P. nigra* subsp. *laricio*),
like many of the trees in this group, have the ability to magnify the sound of
the breeze dramatically. In Japan the pine and the bamboo, both excellent
wind "instruments", are revered.

Too much wind disrupts the positive energy or atmosphere of the
garden and, in very exposed sites, protection in the form of a deep shelter-
belt of mixed tree saplings, filled in with shrubbery and backed by
windbreak mesh, is recommended. Hedges of beech or hornbeam also
make good wind filters, whereas fences and walls often cause even greater
destructive turbulence.

mood music

Musical and often highly ornamental devices have become very popular in the last few years, as interest in Eastern design and philosophy has grown.

ABOVE Water tinkling against metal makes a gentle, persistent sound in this futuristic garden feature.

OPPOSITE PAGE Some wind chimes are beautifully tuned by their creators so that no matter in what order the tubes are struck as they move about in the wind, the music is always pleasing to the ear. Avoid conflicting melodies and disharmony by hanging up only one wind chime within earshot.

Following the principles of feng shui, wind chimes can be used to relieve areas of "stagnant" energy, since they are believed to generate positive energy or chi. They usually consist of a circle of hollow tubes with a central clanger, but the tubes may also be arranged in a straight line, like panpipes. Wind chimes are made in a wide range of metals including copper and stainless steel, and depending on the width and length of the tubes, they generate a clear bell-like tinkling or ringing tone. A variation on the theme is to hang strings of tiny Indian or Tibetan bells that produce a shimmering ringing tone when disturbed. Ceramic wind chimes are also available, but wood or bamboo are more usual and these make low resonant notes, rather like those produced by a xylophone, which can sound like water lapping against the side of a wooden boat.

Before introducing wind chimes, you need to consider a few practical things. Make sure those you choose are suitable for outdoor use and be prepared to rethread the tubes with nylon fishing twine, since some threads will perish very quickly.

Test as many different kinds as you can before making your selection. The appreciation of sound is personal and you need to be sure that you will be relaxed, not irritated, by hearing the tones over and over. Not everyone enjoys the music of wind chimes so check with your neighbours that the sound does not intrude on their peace and quiet, and as a safeguard, try to position them well within the garden boundaries. Do not put loud chimes in a very windy spot close to the house, or you may find that your sleep is disturbed.

BELOW Moving water is a typical feature of a traditional Japanese garden. A guest would stoop to wash their hands in the stone basin, which is constantly replenished, before entering the tea house.

cascades of water

One of the most pleasurable sounds in the garden is that of quickly moving water. Fast-flowing "white" water has a wonderful energy about it that is stimulating and refreshing.

Just listening to the water gushing, splashing and bubbling conjures up images of mountain torrents, crystal-clear springs bursting from the rock face and breathtaking waterfalls. You probably would not create a feature of this nature if you wanted to generate a relaxing and contemplative atmosphere – cascades and geysers have more to do with adding drama and excitement – but you could use the sound of water to mask background noise.

Being able to hear water hidden from view creates intrigue, drawing the visitor on to discover the source. Sound is directional and it is possible in a larger garden to block the noise of water with a rock wall or earth mound so that you come across it by surprise; the face of a mythical creature spouting water into a pool is perfect for a secret grotto.

If space is limited, other options include simple fountain attachments that fit directly on to the outlet of a pond pump. The results tend to be quite soft and gentle, but passing the water up through a fountain sculpture with a number of tiers and outlets magnifies the effect considerably, provided the pump is sufficiently powerful. A more natural alternative is to pump water up through a straight piece of tubing, so that the water jets up above the pool surface then tumbles back down. Special attachments that mimic the surging upwellings of a geyser are great fun and can be incorporated into a cobble "spring" with a hidden underground reservoir. This arrangement is safe for children and looks attractive surrounded by lush planting.

a gentle trickle

Water moving slowly has a soothing, persistent sound, whether it is flowing from a natural watercourse into a wildlife pond or bubbling gently from a jar in a water feature on a patio.

Close to the house, and in areas where you want to sit or entertain, the sound of moving water should be quiet and gentle, fading into the background noises of the garden. Wall-mask fountains such as the traditional lion's head are popular in formal and Mediterranean-style gardens – in a romantic cottage garden you might use an old hand pump fitted into a barrel. But water gushing on to the surface of the pool can make a hollow and artificial noise, so alter the flow rate to obtain a fine stream and a gentle sound. Sometimes all that is needed is a few large cobbles to break the fall of the water.

ABOVE LEFT *If you have the space, you can create a natural-looking artificial stream, though it will need careful planning and construction to appear convincing. The shallow, pebbled edges will attract a host of wildlife.*

You can now buy a wide selection of small self-contained water features such as drilled pebbles and abstract and figurative water sculptures in metal, ceramic or reconstituted stone. They are ideal for incorporating into patios and decks and are usually safe for young children. These use tiny submersible pumps and simply plug in to a convenient power supply. Some run off a transformer, so are safe and relatively easy to install. The components are also available separately so that you can construct your own design, creating a larger reservoir or positioning the sculpture, drilled rock or millstone in an existing pool.

Another subtle way to introduce the sound of gently falling water is with interlocking raised pools where a fine curtain overflows into the lower sections. In a formal setting, you could construct a narrow channel or rill that feeds into a pond.

The traditional Japanese stone drinking bowl or "tsukubai" makes a beautiful trickling sound as it fills continuously with water fed from a bamboo pipe. Although usually supplied with fresh water that overflows the bowl and drains away, you can create the same effect by setting the tsukubai over a hidden reservoir camouflaged with cobbles. A submersible pump continually feeds water back up through to the bamboo inlet pipe. This arrangement would be perfect for a shady moss and fern corner beneath trees.

ABOVE RIGHT *Different grades of gravel, pebbles and cobbles produce a streamside effect and, along with lush planting, help to camouflage the liner of this small pool. The water is pumped up to the higher level and trickles down through the stones, gently bubbling into the pool.*

the laughter of children

Young children love to help out in the garden. Encourage them to join in by giving them their own set of tools: a mini trowel and hand fork, wheelbarrow, watering can, even a toy lawnmower.

ABOVE *The garden represents freedom for children – a place to run around barefoot and blow off steam! Quieter moments come through investigating plants.*

Little ones do not necessarily need a plot of their own, just a few pots on the patio filled with bulbs or hardy annuals that they have planted. Stick in some giant plastic flowers or windmills while they are waiting for things to get interesting. Toddlers will be happy to play by themselves in a sandpit with bucket and spade: build one into an all-weather surface such as the patio close to the house so that you can keep an eye on things – the pit can always be converted to a pool or planter later on. If you construct a pergola over it you can attach shading in hot weather, or even rig up a covering to keep the rain off.

ABOVE *Children often imagine the garden to be enchanted, and figures like this bronze flower fairy will delight them. Animal sculptures also have great appeal.*

ABOVE *Rig up a
swing in a tree, or for
older children, try
making balancing beams
of reclaimed wood or
set logs in the ground
at varying heights like
organ pipes for them to
climb on.*

The garden is an ideal place for kids to free their imaginations and act out different scenarios. A child's sense of scale is very different from our own, and plants such as giant sunflowers that tower above them can seem to come straight out of wonderland. Tents and play houses are great, but children will also happily adopt an ordinary shed or an overgrown part of the garden as their private camp, weaving it into their fantasy world.

Children are drawn irresistibly to water, but the shallowest pool can be highly dangerous. It's wise to stick to a water feature with an underground or hidden reservoir, such as a "geyser" that spurts water randomly. Make the garden more child-friendly by avoiding plants with really prickly leaves, which can be quite nasty to run into or tread on with bare feet. Stone chippings and slate shards are not very forgiving if children fall over, and gravel and chipped bark can be hard going when you are trying to pedal your tricycle. Provide a smooth surface for wheeled toys, but you could also lay out narrow paths that wind through shrubbery or giant-leaved herbaceous plants and tall grasses. Here you can use an exciting range of surfacing materials such as log slices or stepping-stones, and add fairytale figures peeping out of the greenery. If you have room, you could set up a climbing frame or slide, but a simple swing will prove popular with all ages.

the sound of footsteps

The sounds of industry and activity in the garden can be quite reassuring and restful to listen to, especially when it means someone else is doing all the hard work.

BELOW The sounds of young children playing in the garden add to the atmosphere of fun and relaxation. Make some pathways firm and level for careful pedalling.

Most of the regular maintenance that needs to be done in the garden – provided it doesn't involve power tools – generates gentle, repetitive sounds. They may remind you of carefree moments in childhood when you played in the warm sunshine while the adults worked. The regularity and rhythm of certain jobs can be especially relaxing to listen to, whether you are making the sound or just listening to it. Think of clipping a hedge with hand shears and sweeping up the clippings afterwards; hoeing the ground or raking autumn leaves from the lawn. Even the persistent squeak of a wheelbarrow in need of some oil can bring a smile to your face. The soft push-pull purr of an old-fashioned, hand-operated lawnmower instantly transports us back to the days before the advent of noisy electric and petrol-powered machines.

The crunching sound of footsteps on gravel, stone chippings or slate shards can be quite pleasing, but it also acts as a useful security device – burglars like to tread silently. For less sinister reasons, being able to hear a person's footsteps acts as an early warning system, giving you notice of their approach and avoiding a sudden shock if you've been dozing on the terrace. You could also fix a bell to a garden gate if visitors often arrive by this route and you want to have some notice of their approach.

OPPOSITE PAGE Some lawnmowers, especially hand-operated kinds, purr along nicely. Keeping garden machinery well maintained and running smoothly reduces noise nuisance.

BELOW LEFT Signs of industry: a wheelbarrow full to the brim with plant material destined for the compost heap shows that someone has been busy.

a quiet sanctuary

When you just want to get away from it all, escape into your own garden for a little peace and quiet. Create a secluded corner where you can sit and dream.

ABOVE *This pair of white wrought iron chairs set in the shade of a tree creates an invitation to sit and absorb the atmosphere of the garden. Try to find at least one secluded spot for a permanent sitting place.*

You may want some peace and quiet outside, or perhaps you want to enjoy a civilized adult conversation while the children are rampaging around the house. Even within the confines of a relatively small garden, you can often find space for a small nook with a couple of chairs or a bench, and create at least the illusion of privacy. Filter the view of the house and surrounding buildings by encircling your private space with tall evergreen plants such as bamboos and *Elaeagnus* x *ebbingei*. Alternatively create an outdoor room under a vine-covered pergola, with "walls" made of trellis and fragrant climbers.

Traffic noise, as well as fumes, from a road passing near the garden can sometimes be quite intrusive, but plants make an excellent sound barrier, especially a deep border of mostly evergreen shrubs with an intermingling of ornamental trees. The foliage absorbs much of the sound and also filters particles from the air. Even with screens and barriers in place, you may still be conscious of unwanted noise such as the drone of a lawnmower, children playing or dogs barking. In these cases you may find it soothing to have a more pleasing sound in the foreground of your consciousness, such as a trickling water feature or a wind chime.

In traditional Japanese gardens the route that leads away from the main building through the garden to the Tea House is known as the dewy path. At the start, the planting and paving is typical of any cultivated plot, but as you pass through a series of gateways, the atmosphere gradually changes and it is as though you are moving into the wild countryside: the landscape becomes more natural and the paving breaks down to become rough stepping stones. This short journey is symbolic. You leave your worldly cares behind and enter a more peaceful and spiritual realm where you feel closer to nature. The dewy path could easily be modified for Western gardens, helping to calm the mind on the way to a summerhouse or bower.

You can incorporate other elements of Japanese gardens to imbue your outdoor sanctuary with a more restful atmosphere. Key factors are simplicity of design and colour, seen in its purest form in the Zen dry garden or *karesansui* with its expanses of racked gravel, and rock formations rising like islands in a tranquil sea. The only contrast here is the green of carefully trained and clipped evergreen shrubs, and mosses covering the stones. Most people prefer something less austere but limiting the number of garden features, using broad flowing curves and restricting the palette to "quiet" shades, creates an uncluttered and peaceful space.

OPPOSITE ABOVE LEFT *The family dog sniffs the air as it pauses before leaving the enclosure of this shady sanctuary.*

OPPOSITE ABOVE RIGHT *Cats love to sun themselves in the garden and will often have a favourite spot marked out where they won't be disturbed. The sight of them sleeping adds to the air of indolence.*

OPPOSITE BELOW *Rose-covered treillage and lush planting surrounds this terrace, creating a secluded spot for a private conversation.*

taste

Freshly picked home-grown produce is bursting with flavour and vitality. Indulge yourself with succulent
fruits and berries, crisp salads, tangy tomatoes, fresh herbs and even delicate edible flowers.

home-grown delights

Plan your plantings of fruit and vegetables to make them doubly satisfying: they'll be decorative to look at while they're growing and delicious to eat when you harvest them.

Whether you just want to pop outside and gather a handful of fragrant herbs from pots by the back door, or plan whole meals around what is ready for picking each day, growing your own vegetables and fruit can be profoundly fulfilling. You know how much goodness and flavour they contain, and best of all you know that everything is wonderfully fresh and full of vitality and natural sweetness.

Many of the more unusual varieties, including old-fashioned types that are no longer commercially grown, are quite beautiful to look at and handle, with curious shapes,

ABOVE *When you cut through the stem of a plant, pluck its fruits or pull it from the ground, the smell can be really powerful and you can immediately imagine what it will taste like. Growing your own vegetables opens up a new world of flavours and textures. All the produce you harvest from your garden is naturally super-fresh and there is much more variety.*

textures and colours. Despite all the produce that is flown in from around the world, we see the same varieties time and again in shops and supermarkets. When you grow fruit and vegetables in the garden, you can choose cultivars for their outstanding flavour, rather than worrying about the size of the fruit, how easily it can be transported or whether it can be harvested by a machine. If you source seed and plants from specialist growers, you will quickly discover that there is an amazing range available. What matters is not reaching specific production targets, but the experience of producing wholesome, delicious food: replenishing and caring for the soil, raising plants from seed, tending the plot and watching the various crops develop, mature and ripen through the year. The act of harvesting provides plenty of stimulus for the senses and searching through the foliage to see if the crop is ready is very much part of the pleasure of growing your own.

You do not need to have a separate vegetable plot to grow your own. Sowing small patches or short rows of crops amongst the flowering plants can be enough to keep you supplied with fresh vegetables throughout the summer. You can even grow top fruit, strawberries, climbing vegetables and quick-maturing salads in containers on a tiny balcony or backyard patio.

fruit-laden boughs

An orchard in spring or autumn is a magical sight, but few of us have enough space for one. Fortunately, no matter how small your garden, you should be able to squeeze in a few fruit trees.

Biting into a crisp, sun-warmed apple that you have just picked from your own tree is pure pleasure, and even the smallest garden can accommodate an apple tree or two. Both apples and pears make beautiful specimen trees in a lawn, smothered in blossom in spring and gaining character as they age. If space is really limited, train some trees as cordons (single unbranched stems set at a 45-degree angle and grown on wire supports) or make use of walls and fences by growing fan-trained or espaliered fruit trees, the latter having branches in horizontal tiers. Pre-trained forms are available but young trees are cheaper and more vigorous, establish better and can be trained in any shape you require. Some varieties are self-fertile but many require cross-pollination by at least one compatible blossom tree. For apples you can use the crab apple, *Malus* x *zumi* var. *calorcarpa* 'Golden Hornet', which is also very decorative and compact. Apples, cherries, plums and apricots grafted on dwarfing rootstocks take up little room and most can even be grown in tubs, so they are ideal for small spaces.

If you live in a cold, exposed region, late frosts can nip the blossom and prevent the formation of fruit. Seek local advice about types that do well in your area or grow late-flowering varieties and train them against a warm wall, draping the blossom with fleece on cold nights. Birds are troublesome to fruits such as plums, stripping the flower buds, but wall-training allows plants to be netted in during the crucial winter and early spring period.

The early-flowering varieties of dessert apple, such as 'Discovery' and 'James Grieve', produce the first fruit but it needs to be eaten straight away. Later varieties such as the russet apple 'Ashmead's Kernel' and 'Suntan' store well, so that you can continue to eat your crop throughout the winter.

Peaches and nectarines can be prone to disease and are not very hardy, but by fan-training them on a warm wall (using semi-dwarfing rootstocks) or growing in containers (using dwarfing rootstocks), you can combat most difficulties. Plums can be treated similarly, as can apricots: even if you live in an area mild enough to grow them they will benefit from the shelter of a warm, sunny wall. If you want to grow sweet cherries in a small garden, choose the self-fertile 'Stella' for a sunny wall, and for cooking, grow the acid cherry 'Morello', which is happy on a wall that receives little sun. Net the fruit or the birds will beat you to it.

ABOVE *Pears bloom early so are vulnerable to frost, and they also enjoy warmth so are best grown as espaliers or fans against a warm wall or fence. Consult local experts for the best varieties to choose. Early-flowering types include 'Conference' and the old variety 'Williams Bon Chrétien', and for later flowering, 'Doyenné du Comice' and 'Onward'.*

OPPOSITE *If space is limited, train apples as cordons against a wall, fence or trellis.*

succulent soft fruits

Picking a sun-warmed fig and biting into its soft, juicy, sweet flesh is sheer indulgence. Soft fruits capture the essence of a perfect summer's day — and their flavour is all the better for being home-grown.

Fruit that can be eaten straight from the plant epitomizes summer in the garden. You can nibble a few strawberries as you wander around the borders checking on their progress, or send one of the children outside with a bowl before supper to gather the fruit for an instant dessert. Soft fruits, such as strawberries, little aromatic *fraises des bois*, raspberries, figs and grapes are also beautiful to look at and rewarding to grow. If you have acid soil rich in organic matter, the delectable blueberry should do well. Even in a small garden there's sure to be room for a few strawberry plants. They are quite pretty enough to grow in the

flower border, although this may make it more difficult to protect them from slugs and birds. They are easier to net if they are planted in a row, so you could try growing them as edging plants. Buy certified virus-free stock and replant after about the third year of cropping. Plant them in well-manured ground in mid- to late summer, and they will fruit the following year. The season starts with varieties such as 'Idyl', moving on to 'Elsanta' and 'Hapil', then 'Pandora' and the autumn-fruiting 'Aromel'. Grow 'Pandora' with other strawberries to ensure pollination.

For delicious summer-fruiting raspberries, plant varieties such as 'Glen Prosen' and the late-fruiting 'Malling Leo' in autumn or winter, and trim the canes to about 15cm/6in. In spring, tie the strong growths to post and wire supports, and after fruiting cut out these canes to make way for the fresh growth appearing from the base. You can also grow the autumn-fruiting variety 'Autumn Bliss' which is pruned simply by cutting all the canes to ground level in early spring. Feed and mulch both kinds around this time.

Fig trees need a warm wall. Restrict their roots or they will grow enormous before bearing fruit. Briar fruits are rampant and take up a lot of room, but the fruits are delicious. Consider the blackberry 'Ashton Cross', the thornless loganberry 'LY654' or a tayberry.

tangy delights

Rhubarb and gooseberries are some of the first crops in the garden, and their zingy fruitiness suits the freshness of spring and early summer. Jewel-like currants take up this sharp theme.

BELOW *Gooseberries, one of the first fruits of the summer, can be eaten raw if they are allowed to ripen sufficiently before picking, but most people relish the slight sharpness of gooseberries in cooked desserts and sauces.*

Before the balmy days of summer when the garden is full of soft fruit ready to eat, the year's earlier treats need to be cooked to enjoy their intense, clean flavours. Of these, the first is rhubarb. Once established, rhubarb can be forced to crop very early in spring, and the delicate pink stems taste as fresh as the breezes blowing away the winter blues. Rhubarb is easy to grow, though it takes up quite a lot of space. Plant it in winter, with the dormant crown just above soil level, and do not harvest until the second year. Allow the plants to build up by cutting just a few stems in the first couple of years, and don't force the same plants in successive seasons.

Depending on variety, gooseberries may have white, yellow, pink, red or green fruits, with different levels of sweetness. If they are left to ripen fully, the fruits can be eaten straight off the plant. Choose virus-free, mildew-resistant varieties, such as the yellow-fruited 'Jubilee'. The thorny bushes become tangled and congested if left to their own devices, so prune in winter, aiming to keep the centre open. Growing on a short leg makes weeding round the base easier, or they can be trained as double or triple cordons. Another attractive method in a small garden is to grow gooseberries as short standards, and these can make impressive centrepieces for the beds in a formal potager.

Redcurrants such as the variety 'Redlake' are sufficiently sweet and succulent to eat straight off the plant and have a delicate flavour. You can use them to make clear redcurrant jelly, but the fresh fruits are so glistening and beautifully translucent that it seems a shame to process them in any way. As the plants can be grown as cordons, they are ideal for the smallest garden.

The best varieties of blackcurrants have large sweet fruits and good disease resistance. Buy one-year-old plants of certified virus-free stock, such as the compact-growing 'Ben Sarek' and 'Ben More' (the latter is suitable for colder regions). Plant deeply in well-manured soil in winter. Cut these young plants back to just above ground level so that in spring the bushes will grow a good framework of branches. The following year, the blackcurrants will fruit, and to enable you to pick the currants in comfort, you can simply cut the fruit-bearing stems off close to ground level. New stems will develop to produce a crop the following season.

ABOVE *For an early crop of rhubarb try 'Early Victoria' and cut it in mid- to late spring. For a main crop 'Cawood Delight' can be cut in late spring to early summer, or for a late crop 'Strawberry Rhubarb' can be cut in midsummer to early autumn.*

tomatoes and cucumbers

Cherry tomatoes eaten straight from the plant are like little taste explosions with a delicious intensity and sweetness, and home-grown cucumbers have an exceptional flavour.

ABOVE *Grown well, cucumbers produce beautifully sweet, juicy fruits. Some, such as 'Petita F1', are conveniently small. Plant them in well-manured ground and train up a cane wigwam.*

Look in the seed catalogues and you will be amazed at the range of tomato varieties now available. There are disease-resistant varieties, ones for growing exclusively in the greenhouse, others that can also be tried outdoors in a sheltered spot, and more hardy kinds that mature sufficiently early for the crop to ripen before the weather turns. Shape and size vary too. Starting at the small end of the scale there are little plum types such as 'Santa'; ones with pear-shaped fruits, for example, 'Red or Yellow Pear'; and cherry tomatoes, like the pale orange 'Golden Sunrise' or glossy red 'Super Sweet 100'. Cocktail types such as the yellow 'Ildi' look more like grapes and are formed on huge trusses. All of these require even and plentiful watering to promote fruit set and to prevent the tomatoes from dropping prematurely. Larger tomatoes include plum types like 'Roma', beefsteak tomatoes such as 'Marmande' and regular tomatoes such as the high-performing greenhouse variety, 'Shirley'.

Greenhouse varieties tend to be cordon types, which need tying in with soft twine to 1.8m/6ft cane supports. You will also need to pinch out the side shoots to maintain a single stem. There are bush varieties for outdoors that need only a little support, and others that are intermediate in character. Plant outdoors after all risk of frost has passed. Grow tomatoes in 25cm/10in plastic pots or in growing bags following the manufacturer's instructions. Begin feeding with liquid fertilizer when the first fruits have set.

Ridge cucumbers, such as 'Burpless Tasty Green F1', can be grown quite easily outdoors. The newer varieties that do not require much training have made growing cucumbers in the greenhouse easier too. In the past the male flowers had to be removed to prevent fertilization, which made the fruits bitter, but most greenhouse F1 hybrid varieties now remain all-female unless the plants are put under stress. Sow the flat seeds on edge in 7.5cm/3in pots of multipurpose compost (soil mix) in a heated propagator about four weeks before your proposed planting date. In the greenhouse grow F1 hybrids in pots or growing bags and simply tie in to a cane support. Feed every two weeks with liquid tomato fertilizer as the first fruits develop.

BELOW *If you've never grown tomatoes, you'll be surprised at how easy it is to have success with them. Buy young plants or grow them from seed in spring, using 7.5cm/3in pots or a divided tray with one seed per cell to avoid root disturbance when potting on. An unheated windowsill propagator should give sufficient warmth.*

salad days

The beauty of salad vegetables is that they are easy to grow and quick to mature.
You can literally eat what you've sown or planted in a matter of weeks.

Fast maturing crops make useful space-fillers anywhere in the garden, and taste delicious when picked young and tossed straight into a salad or a stir-fry. Speedy salad crops include lettuce, the peppery-flavoured rocket (arugula) – which will seed around the garden by itself if you let it flower – salad onions and radishes. You can also grow succulent baby vegetables in no time, such as young spinach leaves, baby carrots, golf-ball-sized beetroot (beets) and new potatoes. All these, as well as quick herbs such as coriander (cilantro), basil, parsley and chives, can be worked into gaps in the flower border or grown in containers on the patio. Most of the plants, including carrots with their ferny tops, red-veined beet leaves and the fancy lettuce varieties, are quite pretty enough to justify their place in a flower border.

Several salad crops can be grown using the cut-and-come-again technique. For this method choose lettuce varieties that do not produce a solid heart and are slow to run to seed, and those described as leaf-lettuce varieties. Look for 'Saladisi' and 'Valmaine' and try 'Red Salad Bowl' and, perhaps surprisingly, 'Cos'. Cut the young leaves of close-sown, broadcast lettuce, spinach, leaf chicory, rocket and parsley a little above ground level, so that the stumps can continue to grow and produce more leaves. Make

BELOW RIGHT *Beetroot
(beets) can be sown in
early spring under cloches,
and you can make repeat
sowings every few weeks
until the middle of
summer to ensure a more
continuous supply of
young beets. Patches could
easily be grown amongst
bedding and other flowers
for foliage contrast.*

repeat sowings every few weeks to ensure continued cropping. You can also start
vegetables off in small pots or trays to plant out as soon as space becomes available.

For sweet, flavoursome baby carrots use quick-maturing varieties such as 'Amsterdam
Forcing', 'Early Nantes', 'Junior F1' and 'Amini'. You can sow in late winter if you
warm up the seedbed under black plastic sheeting or cloches, so you'll get crops from
late spring. Growing carrots in patches in the flower borders, surrounded by taller
plants, makes it harder for the low-flying carrot root fly to home in on its target.

Salad onions, such as the
popular 'White Lisbon', are
sown direct in the ground
between late winter and
mid-spring, with the first
sowings ready for harvest in
mid-spring. You can also
make successive sowings of
summer-cropping radish
varieties such as 'Cherry
Belle' between midwinter
and late summer, picking
the crop when young and
sweet, and without a hint of
woodiness. For baby beets,
pick quick-maturing
varieties such as 'Boltardy'
and 'Early Wonder' and sow
into pockets of deep soil
rich in organic matter. Pass
the seed under running
water to wash out the
germination inhibitor
and encourage rapid
germination. The leaves are
ornamental, especially when
young, being flushed purple
with a contrasting red
midrib and veins.

peas and beans

These are some of the most worthwhile vegetables to grow, because the taste of freshly picked young peas and beans is far superior to anything you can buy.

ABOVE *French (green) beans may be dwarf and bushy or climbing (supported with canes). Go for stringless varieties with flat or pencil-shaped pods. Some have attractive purple pods such as 'Purple Tepee' or 'Royalty'.*

RIGHT *Some pea and bean varieties are so compact that you can grow them in tubs on the patio. Push in a few twiggy sticks for support.*

Not only are peas and beans tasty and attractive but they also fix nitrogen in the soil, improving its fertility. The earliest to crop is the broad (fava) bean: harvest the green or white beans when they are not much bigger than your little fingernail and they will be sweet, slightly nutty and very, very tender. The plants are remarkably hardy and you can start sowings under glass with cold-tolerant varieties such as 'Super Aquadulce' or 'The Sutton' (a dwarf variety) as early as midwinter. Use small pots or divided seed trays and once they have a couple of good leaves plant them out under cloches. Further sowings give a succession of beans. Use varieties such as 'Bunyard's Exhibition', 'Imperial Green Longpod' and 'Masterpiece Green Longpod'.

The first crops of peas come from late winter sowings using first early varieties such as 'Feltham First' and 'Meteor'. A neat trick is to sow in lengths of drainpipe cut in half so that you can slide the plants and intact root system into the drill when the weather is favourable. Continued cropping comes from second earlies, sown in the same period (late winter to mid-spring), which take a little longer to mature and include 'Hurst Greenshaft' and 'Kelvedon Wonder', followed by maincrop peas such as 'Cavalier'. Many modern pea varieties are short-growing and need little support.

Pea and bean plants are sensitive to low temperatures and slug damage, so insure against loss by raising seedlings in pots in the heated greenhouse in late winter or early spring. Plant them out after hardening off in late spring or early summer. When cropping begins it is best to go out every day to pick the next fresh batch of young flavoursome pods for immediate consumption.

Runner (stick) beans, with their red or white flowers, are very pretty and can be grown over arches and up trellis panels. Since the young beans are so sweet, tender and prolific, varieties such as 'Galaxy', 'Polestar' or 'Mergoles' are well worth trying. They can even be grown in large tubs using a wigwam of canes for support. Harvest regularly, removing over-large pods that have been missed, to maintain cropping. Sow in pots in the greenhouse or on the windowsill in early spring and plant against supports after the risk of frost has passed. Protect French (green) and runner beans with horticultural fleece if cold weather threatens.

OPPOSITE *One of the pleasures of picking peas is popping open the pod, smelling the fresh aroma and sampling the deliciously sweet contents. If you don't have much room, grow one of the gourmet peas such as the mangetout (snow pea) 'Carouby de Maussane' and 'Oregon Sugar Pod' or 'Sugar Snap', the latter eaten as mangetout or peas.*

the squash family

With their exotic-looking golden-yellow blooms and unusually shaped fruits, the squashes are really decorative garden plants, and both fruits and flowers are delicious too.

OPPOSITE *There is a wide range of courgette (zucchini), squash and pumpkin varieties. These yellow-fruited courgettes and orange-skinned squashes are ornamental types.*

BELOW RIGHT *Pumpkins and squashes are best ripened in the sun raised off the damp earth so that they store well. In autumn the sight of this attractive harvest gives tremendous satisfaction.*

The rampant growth of courgettes (zucchini) means that the plants take up a lot of space, but you probably only need a couple to provide enough fruits in season, and you can grow them vertically over sturdy arches or pergolas. Growing your own means that you can pick the fruits when they are really small – not more than 10cm/4in long – and full of flavour. Once the plant starts to fruit, the crop needs to be checked daily, since reasonably sized courgettes seem to be able to blow up into huge marrows almost overnight. As well as the usual green courgettes you can grow the more unusual yellow-fruited varieties, such as 'Gold Rush'.

When you grow courgettes and other squashes you can also eat the beautiful yellow flowers. They can be stuffed, dipped in batter and fried. Pick the male flowers so your crop is not diminished (the females have the beginnings of the fruit behind the flower).

Summer and winter squashes also have ornamental fruits. Summer types such as the pale green 'Patty Pan' and yellow 'Sunburst' have scalloped fruits which can be eaten raw when young, or boiled or stuffed. Winter types such as 'Butternut', which has orange flesh, and the orange-red, ball-fruited 'Uchiki Kuri' store well. The flesh can be boiled and mashed with butter and seasoning or cut into chunks and roasted.

Sow courgettes and squashes in 7.5cm/3in pots in warmth during mid-spring, planting them out into well-manured soil after the risk of frost has passed.

ABOVE *Winter squash is full of beta-carotene, has a sweet, nutty taste, and because of its firm flesh, is easily stored outdoors. Once they are ripe, raise pumpkins or squashes off the damp earth to prevent rotting.*

gourmet selections

Some of the most challenging vegetables to grow are also the most delicious, so if you have the time to spare, they are well worth trying as a special treat.

BELOW *Fennel can be sliced raw into salads, used to make soup or roasted whole.*

BELOW CENTRE *Ruby chard, a dramatic red-stemmed form of Swiss chard, looks fabulous in the flower border and tastes like a superior form of spinach. Sow in rich, moisture-retentive soil in shallow drills during mid-spring. A midsummer sowing gives plants for winter cropping.*

Although they are not easy to grow, "bulbs" of the sun-loving Florence fennel have a delicious, subtle aniseed flavour. Make repeat sowings between mid-spring and late summer in deep soil rich in organic matter. Dry conditions cause premature flowering so water well during periods of drought. Earth up the swollen stem bases when they are golf-ball size to keep them sweet.

Another gourmet vegetable that you might like to try is the sculptural globe artichoke – the plant is a worthy addition to any border, and the edible flower heads are a delicious bonus. You can choose to cut them when the buds are the size of golf balls and entirely edible, or wait until they have swollen to full size. Sow a selection such as 'Green Globe' in mid- to late winter in pots under glass, planting out during early to mid-spring for cropping from midsummer to mid-autumn. The plants will continue to crop for about four years.

One of the classic gourmet vegetables is asparagus. In order to enjoy the succulent new shoots, known as tips or spears, you have to exercise a little patience and be prepared to set aside a special bed for a number of years. The first crop cannot be harvested for two years, following planting of one-year-old crowns, but in the meantime the asparagus fern is a pretty addition to the garden.

OPPOSITE *Specialist seed merchants may stock several different varieties of chard, with its highly ornamental white or coloured stems.*

BELOW *Early purple sprouting broccoli, with long, tender, sweet stems the texture of asparagus tips, is definitely one to include. It crops from midwinter to late spring from a mid- to late spring sowing.*

herbs in the garden

Easy to grow, fragrant and pretty in any setting, no garden is complete without a selection of herbs: it's impossible to resist picking a leaf or two as you pass by.

Most herbs have a softness about them, whether in the colour of their flowers and foliage or overall texture, that makes them good "mixers". If you want a scented or aromatic foil for other plants, herbs are ideal. Lavender, for example, is a classic partner for roses, and the misty foliage of bronze fennel will highlight blooms of substance. White-variegated apple mint, *Mentha suaveolens* 'Variegata', is lovely weaving its way among the flowers in a shady border, and the shade-tolerant varieties of lemon balm (*Melissa officinalis*) – the gold-variegated 'Aurea' and yellow leaved 'All Gold' – are highly ornamental, especially at the

ABOVE *You could create an informal look with herbs, for example, marjoram (*Origanum vulgare*), which self-seeds, especially in gravel paths and cracks in paving. Or use a mixture of the many forms of common thyme (*Thymus vulgaris*) and lemon thyme (*Thymus x citriodorus*), which quickly spread out to soften hard surfaces.*

beginning of the season. As with mints, you do need to control their spread. The variegated and coloured leaf forms of many herbs tend to have lost some of their pungency from a culinary standpoint, but it's amazing how much flavour and aroma is still present in the so-called ornamental varieties.

If you do not have a herb or kitchen garden, one way to grow an abundant supply of herbs for cooking is to use them as edgings for borders and pathways. That way you can harvest them even in wet weather. For a formal feel, grow a low hedge of lavender, hyssop, chives or flat leaf parsley. With one or two exceptions, such as mints and lemon balm, which get mildew if kept too dry, most herbs are quite drought-tolerant so you do not have to worry too much if you forget to water potted herbs occasionally.

With sufficient space you could grow a wide variety of plants in a herb garden or potager laid out in a practical yet ornamental fashion, either informally or according to a traditional geometric layout. You will often see old knot-garden plans recommended as a basis for design but avoid making the beds too complex or intricate. Herbs tend to be quite vigorous and can easily overgrow their allotted space or become too congested: a simple potager design will be easier to maintain.

ABOVE *The majority of herbs can be grown in containers on the patio or around the kitchen door. Choose simple terracotta pots or use wicker basket pot covers for a rustic or cottage-garden feel. Herbs also make excellent subjects for hanging baskets, especially if you mix in a few flowers.*

tender and annual herbs

Although most of the popular herbs are perennials and need little attention, there are some that need to be newly grown each year, being either annuals (or biennials) or too tender to survive cold winters.

OPPOSITE Borage is a sun-loving annual whose young leaves and pretty blue flowers are mainly used to decorate summer drinks. It self-seeds but is easily controlled.

BELOW CENTRE Dill (Anethum graveolens) likes a dry, sunny spot. It should be sown in mid-spring and at monthly intervals thereafter, but if you enjoy collecting your own seed, grow it away from fennel or the two will cross pollinate. Dill's finely divided foliage is perfect for garnishing and is commonly used for flavouring fish dishes.

You can buy most herbs as plants from the garden centre in late spring, but if you want to grow more than one or two clumps, it is more economical to raise your own from seed.

If you love Italian food and simple tomato salads, the half-hardy annual sweet basil (*Ocimum basilicum*) is an absolute must-have herb. Sow it in cellular trays or little pots with heat in the greenhouse, just as you would bedding plants. Pot on as necessary and plant only when thoroughly hardened off and all risk of frost has passed. Sweet marjoram (*Origanum majorana*), a tender perennial best grown as an annual, is another essential herb for Italian cooking.

Parsley (*Petroselinum crispum*) needs no introduction. Sow in modules in mid-spring in a shaded cold frame, or in a cool spot in open ground. Water the drill beforehand, sow thinly to avoid having to disturb the plants later and keep the site moist until the seedlings are through. In the same way as parsley, the annual chervil (*Anthriscus cerefolium*) should be sown in drills outdoors in spring with a little shade and plentiful moisture, and thereafter at monthly intervals to ensure a good supply of young, tasty leaves.

Coriander or cilantro (*Coriander sativum*) is a spicy herb that along with rocket (arugula) adds a kick to salads. It is also a prime flavouring for many Thai, Indian and Mexican dishes. Sow this heat-loving herb direct in the ground in late spring or early summer in full sun for a summer harvest.

BELOW Seed suppliers sell all kinds of basil, including sweet, Genovese, Siam Queen, Cinnamon and Holy, as well as highly ornamental purple-leaved varieties.

savoury flowers

If you are willing to experiment you'll find a number of edible flowers that can enhance a tossed green salad and other dishes, adding beautiful colours and unusual flavours.

BELOW *The chocolate-maroon blooms of the hollyhock,* Alcea rosea *'Nigra', would add a touch of drama to a dish.*

Several herb flowers are suitable for use in salads. Use flowers of freshly opened, aromatic oregano heads and blue-flowered hyssop, or the pink chives or white garlic chives, which also make an ideal garnish for a cheese platter. Bright orange or yellow nasturtium flowers can be added whole to a salad for a hot, peppery surprise. For a similar colour boost but a milder flavour, sprinkle in pot marigold petals (*Calendula officinalis*) or even dandelion petals. The thick, textured daylilies (*Hemerocallis*) might seem an odd choice but some have a particularly nutty flavour, and you can even toss in hollyhock blooms. For soups, garnish at the last minute with pot marigold petals that will float on the surface, and for savoury tarts and flans transfer to a plate and decorate the rim with a few sprigs of flowering rosemary or place a nasturtium bloom at the centre. Fish dishes could be garnished with the traditional accompaniment, dill, using both the delicate umbels and feathery foliage.

Use only flowers that you know are edible, and whatever flowers you choose, they should be freshly picked and young, not woody or bitter-tasting. If they are for decorative purposes only, be sure they can be easily removed from the dish.

Finally, one flower that is well known in Mediterranean countries for being a meal in itself belongs to the courgette (zucchini). The flowers are stuffed with soft goat's cheese and herbs, then deep fried in light batter. They taste divine.

OPPOSITE *Welsh onions* (Allium fistulosum) *have hollow stems and leaves that are used like chives or salad onions, but the flowers also make a wonderful savoury garnish.*

BELOW LEFT *Courgette (zucchini) blooms are highly ornamental and can be used when fully open as an exotic garnish or for eating hot as an appetizer. Stuffed with soft cheese and quick-fried, the petals twist obligingly to seal the contents.*

touch

Experience the garden by touching and feeling the myriad shapes and textures created by the plants, to open up a whole new world of sensuality.

the desire to touch

The plant world encompasses almost every possible texture – smooth, spiky, waxy, fluffy – and no one should resist the impulse to reach out and experience this infinite variety.

BELOW *Some flowers and leaves look as though they must be made out of velvet. There is something about a blood-red rose that urges you to stroke its petals.*

The whole body can experience touch. Feet are particularly sensitive yet we rarely allow them freedom to explore. If you wear gloves to garden you may keep your hands clean but you will be denying yourself the simple pleasure of feeling the soil or your own home-made compost crumbling between your fingers. Sometimes the best way to sense the fragility of a flower or downy felting of a leaf is to brush it lightly against your cheek or across your lips. Most of the skin is covered in tiny hairs that are super-sensitive to touch – even a gentle breeze disturbs them, and when we walk through long grasses with bare legs, it feels as though we are being caressed.

In the garden, despite their aggressive looks, we still feel drawn to touch – cautiously – plants like the prickly sea hollies (*Eryngium*) and globe thistles (*Echinops*) to see if they are as ferocious as they appear. The more dramatic the spines, the greater the urge. Other plants such as Iceland poppies, with their tissue-paper petals, seem so delicate that we marvel that they can survive the elements. And the transience of morning glory (*Ipomoea*), whose flowers emerge in the morning and have faded by the afternoon, makes us value them even more, cupping them in our hands as carefully as we might hold a butterfly.

Although plants offer a wide range of interesting tactile experiences there are many other objects and hard surfaces to explore in the garden. Sculpture, for example, with shapes and textures unknown in the plant world, can positively invite touch.

When designing and planting, we tend to look at textural interest and variation mainly from the point of view of aesthetics: how would a rough-hewn piece of rock look sited next to gleaming, smooth cobbles? Opening ourselves up to the possibilities of touch is one way of developing and nurturing our sensitivity and sensuality. Like children exploring their environment, we need to touch everything to appreciate it more fully.

ABOVE *The seed-heads of many grasses are super-soft and fluffy, and we can sense how they will feel even before we've touched them.*

OPPOSITE *Try closing your eyes and feeling not only the changing shapes and textures of a sculpture beneath your fingertips but also the coolness or warmth of the different materials. What will be the most pleasing to the eye – metal, glass, resin, stone or wood?*

smooth

Smoothness suggests both texture and simplicity of form: smooth surfaces in nature, such as large leaves and rounded pebbles, are restful to the eyes and create a feeling of repose.

BELOW *The solid fruits of the crab apple* Malus *'John Downie' look and feel as though they have been carved from wood and then hand-painted.*

Smooth is the opposite of rough, and when these two textures are set side by side, the contrast can be really exciting – an excellent example is the horse chestnut, whose bright green, prickly fruits split open to reveal the polished "conker".

Large, smooth or glossy leaves have pleasing tactile qualities as well as making a dramatic statement. The exotic-looking, hand-shaped leaves of *Fatsia japonica* can measure up to 30cm/12in across. Such theatrical specimens apart, it is generally only when we look carefully at individual buds, leaves, stems and fruits that we notice how perfectly smooth some of them really are. The embryonic form of some flowers is particularly intriguing, for example, the pale green tapered buds of tulips before they start to show colour.

It is the combination of colour, shape and texture that makes fruits so ornamental. The translucent berries of honeysuckle and *Viburnum opulus* are like polished glass beads. As well as the usual reds and oranges there is the violet-coloured berry, *Callicarpa bodinieri* var. *giraldii* 'Profusion'; the amber yellow berries of the rowan, *Sorbus* 'Joseph Rock', and the startling, kingfisher-blue berries of *Clerodendrum trichotomum*.

In contrast to these rounded shapes, there are the strap-like leaves of New Zealand flax (*Phormium*) and long slender "culms" of mature, thicket-forming bamboos. The ultra-smooth shoots of the black bamboo, *Phyllostachys nigra*, look as though they are coated with lacquer – a dramatic contrast to the fluttering green leaflets. Other species and

OPPOSITE *A cluster of bright shiny cotoneaster berries gleams in the winter sunshine. We usually associate a gloss or sheen with man-made materials and the unusual smoothness, reflecting the light, is why certain fruits and berries attract attention.*

BELOW LEFT *Rounded pebbles and cobbles, smoothed by the action of water, are a delight to touch.*

OPPOSITE *This smooth, touchable wooden seat with its flowing lines is perfectly placed.*

BELOW *In a contemporary setting simple objects often work best. You could use a set of glazed ceramic spheres, a large plain jar or a mirrored obelisk. Set them into the planting to emphasize the difference between the shapes and textures, or make an object more of a feature by placing it in its own space.*

cultivars might have blue, gold, green or yellow-striped culms. Some shrubs also have smooth, colourful stems, including the pheasant berry (*Leycesteria formosa*), whose very pale sage-green shoots make a pleasing foil for the purple drooping flower clusters, and the red- or yellow-stemmed dogwoods, which gleam in the winter sunshine.

Tree bark is not noted for its smoothness but certain species have trunks with a silken feel. One of the most telling in the winter landscape is the cherry, *Prunus serrula,* which looks as though someone has wrapped its trunk tightly with strips of polished copper, and is irresistible. The bark of the white-stemmed birch, *Betula utilis* var. *jacquemontii*, feels like satin beneath the peeling strips of discarded "skin", and the same silky smoothness is found in older specimens of the strawberry tree, *Arbutus* x *andrachnoides*, whose cinnamon pink bark peels irregularly. In the snow gum (*Eucalyptus pauciflora* subsp. *niphophila*), the bark is patterned like interlocking jigsaw pieces or snakeskin, and is fascinating to touch.

Skilfully combining plants and man-made features is what makes a garden special. Hand-crafted objects often have a geometric regularity or unnatural smoothness and solidity that makes them stand out from the textured and apparently chaotic mass of foliage and flower. The best example of this is garden sculpture, such as a figure cast in bronze or resin or chiselled from stone, or an abstract piece with similarly pleasing curves. Sculpture and statuary can be quite expensive and it's sometimes hard to find a style to suit your garden, but there are many other ways of introducing intriguing shapes and contrasting textures. The important thing is to place the object in such a way that it invites touch. Give small pieces extra prominence by placing them on a simple plinth or pedestal. For an avant-garde feel, look for decorative elements in shiny metals, glass or coloured acrylic. In a more natural setting try a sinuous, water-worn hunk of driftwood, large cobbles or a smooth boulder. If you are on a tight budget, you could recycle coloured glass bottles in the garden. Line them up on a wall so that the sun shines through them.

Garden centres now stock some beautiful abstract fountains in simple shapes such as spheres, pyramids and shell-like swirls. The combination of water and sleek stone or ceramic is hard to resist so make sure you place such a water feature where you can sit and idly trace the flow with your fingers. A still sheet of water in a formal pool appears smooth until you touch it and will act just like a mirror, reflecting the cloudscape, the surrounding planting and even the moon.

Look for good tactile qualities in garden furniture too, such as a bench made from a heavy piece of reclaimed wood, sanded to feel perfectly smooth and solid beneath the fingertips. In a garden with a modern slant you might want to use a table and chairs in polished metal or, for a Mediterranean feel, you could choose a mosaic-topped table. Incorporate these smooth, sensuous elements to contrast with all the natural textures in your garden.

rough

*Rough textures create a feeling of solidity and strength: the peaks and troughs of tree bark or
a weathered boulder cast strong shadows across the surface, emphasizing its contours.*

OPPOSITE *In the Zen
dry garden or* karesansui,
*rocks are placed with
infinite care: try using a
large, interesting stone as
a natural sculpture.*

BELOW RIGHT *Carefully
trimmed box "hair" has
become an integral part of
this wildly eccentric
sculpture. Clipping and
training evergreen plants
to create abstract or
geometric green sculpture
often creates a rough
surface with similar tactile
qualities to stone.*

Natural rocks are not just for alpine gardens. You can appreciate their rugged texture in
any setting, and they will contribute an architectural element to the garden. They do need
careful placing to fit naturally into the garden landscape and should be bedded into the
ground to make them look as if they belong there. A well-positioned rock or a grouping
of large stones has an imposing presence, set among lower-growing plants or beneath the
arching branches of a tree such as Japanese maple. Alternatively you could compose a
group of three or five large stones, in which the largest acts to anchor the rest. In a
contemplative setting, such as a clearing between trees, you could even construct a
mystical stone circle from tall, upright rocks.

Certain evergreen ground cover plants have a similarly rough and rugged feel,
including many of the prostrate junipers such as *Juniperus communis* 'Green Carpet' and
J. horizontalis 'Blue Carpet'. Prostrate junipers and ground-hugging cotoneasters, like
Cotoneaster congestus and *C. x suecicus* 'Coral Beauty', can also be used to cover banks
and cascade down over retaining walls.

Clipped topiary figures, such as those cut from box, yew or *Lonicera nitida*, are relatively
smooth in outline but satisfyingly rough to the touch. You can also stroke the domes of
small-leaved hebes such as *Hebe rakaiensis*, which keep a tight shape if clipped annually, as
well as any of the regularly shaped dwarf conifers.

BELOW *To enhance
the contrast with a
smooth surface or plants
with simple-shaped
leaves, use the roughness
of gravel, recycled metal
discs or slate shards.*

grooved and crinkled

The pattern of veins in a leaf is part of its individual character and in some plants the veins are so pronounced that the leaf appears puckered, crinkled or ridged.

The massive foliage of the bog plant *Gunnera manicata* is dramatically veined, especially when the new leaves are not yet fully expanded. Many other large-leaved bog plants have deeply textured leaves that give them a similarly sculptural form. They include rodgersias; *Darmera peltata*, the leaves of which are reminiscent of parasols; and the towering ornamental rhubarb, *Rheum palmatum* 'Atrosanguineum'.

Some plants have a distinctly pleated texture, especially when the foliage is young and fresh. The shade-loving connoisseur's plant, *Veratrum nigrum*, produces a clump of

ABOVE LEFT *The hart's tongue fern (Asplenium scolopendrium) has smooth leaves with intriguingly ruffled edges.*

leaves that are folded as sharply as a fan when they start to expand, the parallel veins remaining well defined all season long. Lady's mantle, *Alchemilla mollis*, is not so refined but its scalloped-edged leaves also have fan-like pleats. The surfaces of these leaves repel water and they look magical covered in jewel-like droplets after rain. When the foliage and flowers begin to look tired in midsummer, cut the whole plant back to ground level, feed and water and enjoy a second crop of leaves. This also controls self-seeding.

Certain shrubs have distinctive veining. The dark evergreen foliage of *Viburnum davidii* is made more handsome by its parallel grooves and red leaf-stalks and the large, almost oblong leaves of *Viburnum rhytidophyllum*, each deeply marked with a fine network of veins, make this an architectural specimen. Like all large-leaved plants it prefers to grow in a moderately sheltered place so that the foliage does not tear in the wind. *Hydrangea aspera* 'Villosa' gives a similar effect but its large leaves are velvety.

Most trees have textured bark, and in some species, such as sweet chestnut, old specimens have deeply grooved trunks – wonderful to touch with your eyes closed. By contrast, the trunks of the aptly named snake-barked maples, such as *Acer capilles* and *A. davidii*, are relatively smooth, but appear grooved with markings of white parallel lines.

ABOVE RIGHT *Certain kinds of parsley have frilly foliage due to the wavy edges of its highly dissected leaves. For maximum textural interest choose varieties like 'Moss Curled'.*

softly, softly

Nature produces many different textures, but the quality of softness is unfailingly appealing and whenever we discover a plant species with this feature we tend to seek it out.

OPPOSITE *Soft white downy tufts on cotton grass (*Eriophorum angustifolium*). This bog plant is suitable for planting around wildlife ponds in larger gardens.*

BELOW RIGHT *The strokeable lamb's ears (*Stachys byzantina*) prefers a sunny spot. If you just want the foliage effect, making a soft foil for plants at the front of the border, choose a non-flowering variety such as 'Silver Carpet' or the lime green 'Primrose Heron'.*

Carpeting mosses are possibly as close as you can get to the feel of velvet in the garden, but many leaves and flower petals have a similar quality. Look out for silver leaves: these often have a soft texture since they derive their colour from a layer of light-reflecting hairs. Take the wonderfully named lamb's ears (*Stachys byzantina*), the leaves of which are thickly coated in silken fur and do indeed feel very like the soft ear of a lamb or a rabbit. The leaves of the biennial *Salvia argentea* are similar, though much larger, forming a rosette in the plant's first year. Some of the mulleins are also very soft and touchable: of special note is *Verbascum bombyciferum*, a silver-coloured biennial or short-lived perennial covered in such dense white wool all the way up its statuesque flower stems that you can barely see the flowers. Some silver plants have a more felt-like quality. In *Artemisia stelleriana* 'Boughton Silver', the leaves create a brocade-like pattern and look as if they have been cut from white cloth with a fine pair of scissors.

The yellow lanterns of *Clematis tangutica* are followed by swirling silken seed-heads in autumn, but in other species softness is only apparent after leaf fall. If you look at the stag's horn sumach (*Rhus typhina*) in winter, you will see that its bare "antlers" are covered in down. The wild pussy willow (*Salix caprea*) produces its white fluffy catkins on dark bare stems in spring and its garden variety, 'Kilmarnock', makes a small weeping specimen tree which, if thinned out regularly, displays the showy catkins well.

BELOW *Trail your fingers through the feathery plumes of the aromatic herb fennel.*

Soft feathery textures are found in both leaves and flowers. There are the fluffy, moisture-loving meadowsweets (*Filipendula*) and the soft, tapering plumes of astilbes. Pampas grasses also have plume-like flowers, the shorter growing *Cortaderia selloana* 'Pumila' carrying the creamy heads at a more accessible height. The ornamental grasses as a whole have much to offer. On a smaller scale than pampas grass are the forms of Chinese silver grass (*Miscanthus sinensis*) such as *M.s.* 'Silver Feather' and the slightly tender fountain grasses like *Pennisetum alopecuroides* and *P. villosum,* which have soft arching bottlebrush heads. Some grasses are nothing short of diaphanous. For shimmering clouds in late summer and autumn try *Deschampsia cespitosa* 'Goldschleier' (its name means "golden veil") or the purple moor grass, *Molinia caerulea.*

A similar quality in foliage can be achieved by growing bronze fennel (*Foeniculum vulgare* 'Purpureum') and the finely cut artemisias such as *A.* 'Powis Castle'. Ferns offer a huge range of textures and leaf shapes and some, like *Adiantum pedatum* which closely resembles maidenhair fern, are really delicate. The annual *Cosmos bipinnatus* combines satiny dish-shaped blooms in pink or white with bright green filigree foliage and is a useful filler for gaps in the mixed border. Another annual, love-in-a-mist, is very aptly named, with intricately fashioned sky-blue flowers among a haze of green.

One of the classic plants for mixing with more solid-looking flowers, either in the border or in a bouquet, is the pure white baby's breath, *Gypsophila paniculata.* This is most useful for planting behind oriental poppies, spring bulbs and *Dicentra spectabilis,* so

BELOW Gypsophila *'Rosenschleier'* *('Rosy Veil'), a relative of the common white baby's breath, has tiny pompon blooms shaded palest pink, which are carried on fine stems. It's a lovely plant for producing a romantic effect, especially when teamed with larger sculpted blooms. This kind of airy softness looks best when it is contrasted with larger, solid forms.*

that it can fall forwards and fill the gaps these plants leave as they die down. But at the front of the border try the delightful pink hybrid 'Rosy Veil', which grows to only 30cm/12in. Some of the thalictrums have a similar form, especially *T. delavayi* whose 1.5m/5ft high wiry, branched flower stems are covered in tiny lilac blooms, each with a tuft of yellow stamens. The variety *T.d.* 'Hewitt's Double' produces tiny ball-like rosettes and is equally charming.

Very finely cut foliage is less common in shrubs and such plants tend to need good moisture-retentive soil and protection from wind and strong sunlight to avoid scorching. The Japanese maples of the elegant *Acer palmatum* var. *dissectum* group have exquisitely fine palmate leaves. Some of the elders, such as *Sambucus nigra* f. *laciniata* and *S. racemosa* 'Tenuifolia', have a similar look. The smoke bush, *Cotinus coggygria*, gets its common name from its flowers. These are particularly beautiful on the dark purple-leaved forms and even after the tiny blooms have faded, the plant remains covered with a misty haze. After rain, the fine stems capture the gleaming drops like a spider's web.

Grow all these soft plants close to pathways and let them overhang so that the foliage and flower-heads dangle invitingly. Everyone who walks past will want to let a hand brush through swathes of soft grasses or feathery foliage.

Remember that softness is always appreciated more readily when it is contrasted with hard surfaces or simpler shapes, such as large leaves, that act as a foil. Set off soft specimens with mirrored or glazed surfaces and rough and rugged stone.

BELOW *Most of the taller ornamental grasses, such as the* Pennisetum *pictured, yield to the wind so easily that the slightest breeze causes the fluffy heads to move in gentle waves. This is one reason why grasses work best when planted in swathes rather than as single specimens.*

papery

Not surprisingly, papery textures are most prevalent in autumn when flower-heads fade and dry out on the plants, becoming skeletal. Seed-heads form and foliage begins to wither.

BELOW *Acer griseum, the paper bark maple, is a lovely tree noted for its peeling, papery-thin bark. To appreciate the cinnamon colour, make full use of backlighting.*

In very dry, sunny weather, parts of some plants become so fragile that they seem ready to crumble to dust in your hands. Some seed-heads puff up like Chinese paper lanterns, and these include the annual love-in-a-mist (*Nigella damascena*), and the perennial *Physalis alkekengi* var. *franchetii,* whose bright orange "balloons" make an eye-catching feature in the autumn border. On the bladder senna, *Colutea arborescens* – a useful shrub for poor ground in sun – the inflated papery "pea pods" that follow the flowers are copper-tinted. The common spring-flowering honesty (*Lunaria annua*) gets its Latin name from its flat, moon-like papery seed pods. To reveal the translucent silvery centres, wait until the pods have turned from green to brown and simply rub off the outer coating.

Honesty is just one of several plants that can be cut for dried flower arrangements. Most flowers have to be harvested at their peak and then dried in bundles under cover in an airy environment, but the so-called everlasting flowers already have the required papery texture. Varieties of the annual strawflower, *Helichrysum bracteatum,* such as 'Hot Bikini', have dense double daisy blooms and are easy to raise from seed, as is the sea lavender or statice, *Limonium sinuatum,* which comes in assorted colours.

When trees surround your garden you may dread the autumn, since the job of clearing fallen leaves seems never-ending. But leaf fall is an incredibly beautiful time and few plants actually suffer through being temporarily covered, so you can safely wait until the majority have dropped. It is far more satisfying to do the job all in one go. Get the children or grandchildren to help pile them up for composting and join in the fun when they dive into the heaps of leaves.

At the end of the year you can also enjoy the peeling trunk of a white-stemmed birch such as *Betula utilis* var. *jaquemontii,* which stands out even more dramatically when its branches are bare. Another very good tree for winter effect is the paper bark maple, *Acer griseum,* whose tattered bark remnants glow cinnamon when the tree is backlit by the low winter sun.

ABOVE *Sometimes by arranging quite ordinary items in a particular way we become aware of their special qualities. Here onions hang on a rack to dry.*

OPPOSITE *In a fine autumn, the rounded flower-heads of* Hydrangea macrophylla *cultivars dry like parchment. They often retain some of their original colour, making them invaluable for cutting. But if they are left on the plant they last through the winter, protecting next year's buds and looking magical when covered in hoarfrost.*

waxy

Waxiness is a surprising and exciting texture in nature. Because it is a quality often found in tropical plants, waxy leaves and flowers give the garden an exotic feel.

OPPOSITE ABOVE LEFT
Few flowers have the sculpted quality of the arum lily (Zantedeschia aethiopica). When newly opened and without a blemish, they are exquisitely beautiful; a curious mix of solid and ephemeral. For a serene feel, plant next to a calm reflecting pool.

OPPOSITE BELOW LEFT
The fiery red hot pokers — this one is Kniphofia *'Alcazar' — are so solid and waxy before the individual blooms begin to open, that they look almost artificial. If you want the look of the sub-tropics, these bold plants are a must.*

Succulents and some drought-tolerant shrubs and perennials have very thick leaves and stems, which feel solid and heavy. Flowers can also have a waxy texture, and this is the case with some of the largest and most beautifully sculpted blooms. We find these flowers fascinating to touch, because we are used to petals being very delicate and insubstantial. Some of the simply shaped blooms, like those of the white moisture-loving arum lily, *Zantedeschia aethiopica*, and the colourful hybrids of the tender *Z. rehmannii*, add a dramatic touch, and in particular suit the space-age atmosphere of modern minimalist gardens. If you have room to grow the bog arum (*Lysichiton americanus*), you will be amazed at the size and texture of the spathes that push up through the mud in early spring. This plant is sometimes rather unfairly called the skunk cabbage.

On a smaller scale in the flower border, there are plants like the daylily (*Hemerocallis*) which along with some of the true lilies, such as the apricot-coloured cultivar 'African Queen', have large trumpet-shaped blooms. These work best given a diaphanous backdrop such as gypsophila, *Thalictrum* or bronze fennel. Other members of the lily family, like the towering *Cardiocrinum giganteum*, which prefers dappled shade and moist, humus-rich soil, and the amaryllis family — which includes the exotic-looking crinum and belladonna lilies as well as the familiar daffodil — also produce flowers with a waxy texture.

During winter and early spring, the weather-resistant camellias begin to open their solid, highly structured blooms, surrounded by thick, glossy leaves. The low-growing elephant's ears (*Bergenia*) also generate an impression of substance with their large rounded leaves and stout flower stems bearing thick-textured bells. The waxen buds of *Magnolia* x *soulangeana* cultivars appear like tapered candles at the end of bare branches in mid-spring, but if you want a real talking point, grow the bull bay, *Magnolia grandiflora*. The massive leaves are thick and glossy and the creamy blooms open out wide to around 25cm/10in across.

The fleshy-leaved succulents, including creeping sedums, sempervivum, and the tender echeverias, aeoniums and agave, evoke the Mediterranean in a hot, sunny corner, especially when mixed with colourful geraniums and portulacas. Being drought-tolerant, all are happy in terracotta pots of free-draining compost so you can easily move tender specimens back under cover at the end of the season. In the surrounding borders add architectural plantings of *Euphorbia characias* subsp. *wulfenii*, *Galtonia candicans*, yuccas and flame-coloured red hot pokers — another group with solid waxen flower spikes — as well as taller sedum cultivars including the dark red or maroon forms of *Sedum telephium*.

OPPOSITE ABOVE RIGHT
Succulent foliage plants such as the tender rosette-forming echeverias and hardy houseleeks (Sempervivum), grown in pots on a sun-drenched patio, add a flavour of the Mediterranean. The leaves of drought-resistant plants often have a glaucous blue or silver colouring because of their waxy coating.

OPPOSITE BELOW RIGHT *Surprisingly, each of these large, waxy and rather luscious-looking* Hemerocallis *blooms lasts only a day, hence the common name of day lily.*

spiky

Prickly plants have a fascinating structure and some are quite beautiful. No matter how malevolent they look, our curious nature demands that we investigate by touching them.

Thorns, prickles and bristles may be confined to the stems or, as in the case of the tender *Colletia hystrix* (syn. *C. armata*), can completely cover the plant, making it a study in medieval ferocity. In one shrub rose with the diabolical name of *Rosa sericea* subsp. *omeiensis* f. *pteracantha*, the large red thorns are shaped like shark's fins, and being translucent, are very decorative when the low winter sun shines through them.

Sometimes, as with evergreen berberis, mahonia and holly, leaves are shaped in such a way that the lobes form barbs. The leaves of the aptly named hedgehog holly, *Ilex*

ABOVE *If you have children, thorny plants like this holly should be kept to the back of the border, and you need to take care when weeding around them as they are extremely prickly.*

aquifolium 'Ferox', have spines not only on the leaf margins, but also on the leaf surface. In the extreme example of the barrel cacti, leaves are dispensed with altogether. Sea hollies have a spiny ruff around the flower-head, and in the globe thistle the thorns actually protrude between the petals, ensuring that only pollinating insects such as bees and moths have access.

Many prickly plants, including the globe thistle and bear's breeches (*Acanthus spinosus*), have evolved in very hot, dry environments where grazing is thin on the ground and unprotected juicy shoots and flowers would be a great temptation. Some, like the sea holly (*Eryngium maritimum*), have adapted to the hostile conditions on the seashore, others to the cold, arid conditions of the high mountains.

The drought-resistant nature of many of these plants can be seen in the leathery texture of the foliage and the moisture-conserving coating that often makes them appear silver or blue-grey. Although the more delicate-looking varieties, such as *Eryngium alpinum,* can look attractive in traditional borders, many seem more at home in a gravel garden or mulched with rock shards, mimicking their natural environment. They combine well with narrow-leaved plants such as ornamental grasses, cordyline and *Phormium tenax.*

smooth underfoot

There is nothing quite like going barefoot in the garden. Taking your shoes off outdoors is a gesture of freedom and can feel wonderful.

OPPOSITE *As well as decks built on to the house for dining and lounging, you can also make wooden walkways over water or boardwalks to wind through plantings. These are in keeping with wild, waterside or woodland-style gardens, but in shade, tack on some fine galvanized wire mesh for extra grip. It will not be as comfortable to walk on, but it will be safer, since algae creates a slippery and dangerous surface. Watch out for splinters, too, if the wood is rough.*

RIGHT *Machine-grooved wooden decking is now commonly used as an all-weather alternative to paving. Part of its popularity is due to the way it feels underfoot — warm with a certain amount of give.*

If your work is largely cerebral, or if you are stressed, walking barefoot outside will help you to feel grounded and to put problems into perspective. Some people actually garden in bare feet in the summer, enjoying the direct contact with the earth. Provided you are not using any sharp tools, the main danger will be getting seriously grubby soles, but that is nothing that a long hot bath will not cure.

Try to make it possible to walk barefoot right around the garden. Most people find it difficult to walk on gravel or stone chippings without shoes, but you can always incorporate some smooth stepping stones. Placed slightly further apart than normal they can slow down your pace, forcing you to be mindful of each step. Decking squares are easy to lay in place of stones and they dry out quickly after rain. Because of their mobility, they can be lifted and re-laid at another location with very little effort. You might even create a simple circuit for a walking meditation, drawing your awareness within yourself by focusing on the sensations underfoot.

If you want to create the look of a Zen garden in a large, gravel-surfaced area, use randomly shaped pieces of flat rock, such as slate or sandstone, to provide an easy route through, but make sure the stones are laid in a natural pattern. Sparing plantings put directly into the gravel, such as dwarf pines and evergreen azaleas, ornamental sedges, hostas and iris, will add to the picture.

BELOW *Smooth bricks, or exterior quality tiles, are lovely to walk on barefoot, and a good choice for a patio area.*

tactile for toes

Changing the texture underfoot by using a variety of materials can subtly signal the fact that you are moving into another distinct area of the garden.

OPPOSITE *You can easily imagine walking barefoot out through this open gate along mown paths.*

BELOW *This swirling design of pebbles was created by a leading exponent of mosaic work. But anyone can work a simple mosaic panel into a patio or pathway.*

Most gardens contain contrasting areas of paving and other smooth surfaces such as decking or lawn and you can create plenty of visual and tactile interest by varying these surfaces even more. Perfectly flat paving is an obvious choice for a terrace or patio, but rather than using just one type of paving unit, why not mix in different elements laid in a variety of designs – smooth concrete slabs, slate, riven stone, bricks or granite setts? You could even lay concrete and then push in smooth cobbles to create an undulating surface, or use small coloured pebbles to make a mosaic. Random or crazy paving is another possibility, but this looks best with natural stone rather than broken slabs.

Tiles make a refreshing change from ordinary paving units and would work well for a summer dining area close to the house, perhaps creating a visual link with the kitchen. Use frost-resistant ceramic tiles with a moisture-proof membrane underneath or natural tiles, such as slate, which can be streaked with different shades and look fabulous after rain. Decking warms up quite quickly with some direct sun, even in winter. Just make sure when the boards are laid that the wood is free from splinters.

Children love stepping stones, and you could use tree-trunk slices set into bark chippings or cast stepping stones embossed with animal motifs, flowers or fairies. Another variation is to use lengths of stout reclaimed wood such as old railway sleepers (ties) partly buried in gravel or pebbles. Try staggering them lengthways to make interlinking balancing beams. The kids will really enjoy playing on these, but they also provide visual contrast and look quite contemporary when interplanted with architectural foliage plants.

If you want to feel the sand between your toes, you don't necessarily have to go to the beach. Roll up your trouser legs and get into the sandpit with the children. Make the surroundings more like the seaside with decking or boardwalks surrounded by cobbles and shingle. Add a couple of deckchairs and clumps of the blue dune grass, *Leymus arenarius,* and create your own beach scene. It does not matter how big the sandpit is provided you can cover it completely to keep out cats and prevent leaves and litter blowing in – a canvas tarpaulin is ideal.

Carpets of plants are completely different to walk over, cool and springy and especially nice if they are aromatic. In sun, try the low-

BELOW Erigeron
karvinskianus *is ideal
for colonizing cracks in
paving, softening the look
and feel of the path
or patio.*

growing, non-flowering chamomile called *Chamaemelum nobile* 'Treneague' with its fruity
fragrance, or creeping thymes, but be careful not to step on a bee at flowering time. For a
cool, mossy look in a shady spot, use creeping mint, *Mentha requienii* or the non-scented
mind-your-own-business (*Soleirolia soleirolii*). To avoid plant carpets becoming threadbare,
work in some stepping stones, or simply plant through wide cracks left between paving.
The little daisy-flowered *Erigeron karvinskianus* makes low-spreading hummocks and
flowers all summer long. It will happily seed once one or two plants have been established.

Grass is naturally the most hard-wearing plant to use, and is wonderful to walk on
barefoot at any time. If you have not tried it, feel what it is like to step out on to the grass
after rain; when the dew has come down at dusk, or first thing in the morning. You can
vary the texture of lawns by mowing different areas at slightly different heights. The
designs and patterns can be geometric or swirling, but if you decide you do not like the
effect, it is easy to wipe it out and start again with the next cut. Mow narrow paths in a
semi-wild garden: the tall grasses and wild flowers feel wonderful against bare legs. Cut the
paths regularly to prevent coarse grasses from building up and leaving sharp stems.

For a shady area next to a wall or beneath trees, where lawn grass and other plants
struggle to grow, you might try to create a moss carpet. In time this will feel like velvet

BELOW *Stepping-stones
can create a very evocative
atmosphere. Why have I
come off the main track,
you ask yourself, and
where is this leading to?
Stepping one foot at a
time across an area of
planting, gravel or water
increases your awareness
and slows you down.*

BELOW LEFT *A sandpit surrounded by lawn, smooth paving or decking is ideal for children who love to run around all summer in bare feet. If you're inclined to join in, you can even create a mini-beach with suitable props and planting.*

underfoot. Prepare the ground by removing weeds and working plenty of organic matter into the surface. Provided the ground is kept moist, mosses will soon colonize, creating a gently undulating surface. To avoid disturbing the mosses too much, lay a zig-zagging route across the area using stepping stones of tree-trunk slices or porous rock, such as limestone or sandstone, which the mosses will be able to colonize. If the area is large enough, you could turn it into a traditional Japanese stroll garden, planting the odd fern or Japanese maple and arranging interestingly shaped rocks or a stone lantern.

Children love to play with water and a safe water feature with a fountain or geyser springing up through cobbles can be great fun for them to jump across on a hot day. Adults also like to feel the spray from a fountain and dabble their fingers in a pond, but to cool your heels in summer why not build a small formal pool set into the patio or deck that you can paddle in? Most people are a little squeamish about feeling aquatic plants and creatures around their feet but you could cover the base of the pool with pebbles or glass beads to make the water more inviting. A small fountain or water jet would keep the water moving to prevent stagnation. If you are lucky enough to have a natural stream or a large, natural pool in your garden, then you could build a simple wooden bridge or jetty, where you can sit and dangle your feet in the water.

BELOW RIGHT *During the summer months it would be very tempting to wander barefoot along the grassy bank of this stream and to settle on the wooden bridge with your feet dangling in the water. The sensation of water flowing around you can be deeply relaxing.*

scent

Step out into the garden and breathe in nature's fragrances and aromas: spicy, sweet, tangy, musky…the damp earth itself is a veritable pot pourri.

fragrant moods

Scent has the power to evoke memories, even enabling us to recall moments from childhood, and it undoubtedly affects us on an emotional level.

BELOW *Lonicera 'Graham Thomas' is a selection of the wild woodbine or honeysuckle (*L. periclymenum*) with larger than normal flower-heads and a sweet perfume that pervades the garden on a summer's evening. Try it over a shady arbour.*

Perfumed and aromatic plants enhance the atmosphere of a meditation garden or quiet retreat, and a herb garden might be viewed as your own private aromatherapy salon. You could even create the right ambience for romance with intoxicating, evening-scented blooms such as jasmine, honeysuckle, *Lilium speciosum* and exotic angel's trumpets.

When we come across a beautiful bloom we expect it to be fragrant and are disappointed if it is not. Intoxicating scents and aromas are integral to our enjoyment of the garden and we can create a heady effect by growing a variety of perfumed plants together. And as well as flowers, there are the delicious smells of newly mown grass.

A variety of flower parts are involved in releasing perfumed and aromatic oils. As flowers are designed to attract pollinating insects, the petals, stigma and stamens or the whole flower may be perfumed. Some plants have aromatic leaves that need to be brushed against or crushed to release the oils, while others have aromatic bark, seed pods or fruits.

Sometimes fragrance is elusive and you need to put your nose right into the flower to appreciate its scent. The strength of perfume can also vary during the day and under different atmospheric conditions. Curiously, some winter-blooming plants hardly smell when you are standing by them and yet their perfume can be caught some distance away on the breeze. Fragrance is often more powerful when a flower is picked and brought indoors. A posy of double snowdrops gathered on a cold day with no detectable scent outdoors can fill a warm room with honey sweetness. Roses are similar, and sometimes their fragrance alters, with other notes becoming more prominent as the flower warms up. A few plants are exclusively night-fragrant, including *Cestrum parqui*, while others such as honeysuckle and petunia release more perfume in the evening to attract night-flying moths.

ABOVE *Winter fragrance is unexpected, but certain shrubs, such as witch hazel (*Hamamelis mollis*), the shrubby honeysuckle (*Lonicera fragrantissima*) and Daphne bholua (pictured), have really powerful scents. Plant close to doorways, paths and drives.*

OPPOSITE *The heady perfume of jasmine (*Jasminum officinale*) will waft through doors and windows. This vigorous vine will even climb to the bedroom window.*

the intoxicating rose

The rose is deeply rooted in our psyche as a symbol of spiritual and romantic love — think of the apothecary's rose garden and all the fairytales that involve a blood-red rose.

Roses have an ancient and complex history and their origins are shrouded in myth and legend, adding to their aura of romance. The ancient Greeks and Romans loved the rose and gave it its emblematic association with love and beauty, but the main reason for its popularity in ancient times was its scent. Triumphal processions were scattered with scented rose petals like confetti, and both rose water and the extremely concentrated attar of roses were manufactured. The petals were also dried to make pot pourri.

Sniffing the intense fragrance of ancient species such as *Rosa gallica officinalis*, 'The Apothecary's Rose', or the 'Autumn Damask', *R. x damascena bifera*, we can understand why the rose should have been so loved throughout its long history. The damask roses are thought to contain varieties of Persian origin and some of these have been cultivated for centuries to make rose water and attar of roses. Today, when we think of an evocative, romantic garden setting, we are likely to imagine a rose garden or arbour filled with fragrance. It is because of their delicious perfumes and romantic origins that the old roses still have such a powerful allure, despite the fact that many flower for only a short period, can be ruined by rain and are often difficult to fit into a small garden.

We cannot bear a rose to lack scent, and it is understandable that people think of this as a failing of modern roses. When the main aim of breeding was to produce a neat, floriferous bush rose suitable for bedding schemes and small gardens, or the "perfect" tea rose flower form, scent was sadly neglected. In recent years, however, the situation has changed and you can now choose from an ever-expanding group called the English roses, bred by David Austin in Britain. These look like old roses, but the colour range is much wider and they have good resistance to disease and rain. Unlike many of the old roses, they repeat-flower, and best of all, much of the old perfume has been bred back in.

The diverse group that includes the Old Garden Roses, as well as the early hybrids between European and Oriental

OPPOSITE ABOVE LEFT

The simple blooms of the climber R. 'Mermaid' are highlighted by a central boss of golden stamens. This vigorous, stiffly branched rose, suitable for training up the wall of a large house, will release its perfume readily once the brickwork warms up.

OPPOSITE BELOW LEFT

Spectacular in flower with well-scented clusters of semi-double, creamy white blooms and coppery tinged foliage, R. 'Bobbie James' is a rampant rose that will even clamber up into a tree if given some initial support.

roses, varies considerably in habit, ranging from large lax shrubs with arching branches to climbers and upright bushes that look best when their bare "legs" are camouflaged with perennials and herbs. Some look beautiful when their blooms mingle with others at flowering time, normally around midsummer, and a few, such as the Bourbon roses, of which 'Madame Isaac Pereire' is a powerfully fragrant example, flower again in autumn. Try combining them with ornamental alliums, tall bearded irises and the spires of campanulas, with a backdrop of bronze fennel and cloud-like *Crambe cordifolia*.

Species and shrub roses may have single and semi-double blooms with a large central boss of stamens, but the flower shape that we most associate with old roses is fully double, almost pompom-like or patterned with intricate quartering, as seen in 'Charles de Mills' and 'Cardinal de Richelieu'. The curious moss roses derive their name from the mossy appearance of their buds and stems, caused by a coating of glandular hairs that are fragrant and sticky to touch. The blooms of the moss rose 'William Lobb' are a moody purple with lavender-grey shading and are well-scented.

Still in a romantic vein, there are the rambler roses, many of which are vigorous with long, lax thorny stems that, in the case of *R. filipes* 'Kiftsgate' and others, can be encouraged to scramble up into the branches of a tree. The small single or double blooms are often produced in large clusters and at the peak of flowering seem to smother the plant. Good examples for fragrance include the white-flowered 'Rambling Rector', 'Sander's White Rambler' and 'Seagull'. The lovely light salmon-pink-flowered 'Albertine' also has a good scent that wafts out into the air around it. Modern climbing roses grown for fragrance and repeat-flowering include 'New Dawn', 'Compassion' and 'Breath of Life'.

If you have room for a wide, informal rose hedge, consider the disease-resistant *R. rugosa* group. The highly scented flowers are white, pink or, as in the double-flowered 'Roseraie de l'Hay', deep purple-red. The single varieties have the added bonus of large red hips. The fresh green foliage is a little coarse but the long flowering period makes up for that.

Modern cluster-flowered and patio roses are all repeat-flowering, beginning in mid-spring and continuing after a short break through the autumn. They look wonderful with lower-growing herbaceous plants such as catmint, lady's mantle, herbaceous geraniums, artemisias and penstemons, as well as lavender. The white-flowered, lemon-scented *R.* 'Margaret Merril' is particularly elegant, but also consider 'Deb's Delight', 'Bright Smile', 'English Miss', 'Indian Summer', 'Korresia' and 'Fragrant Delight'.

Some roses are remarkable not for the fragrance of their flowers but for their scented foliage. The eglantine or sweetbriar rose, *Rosa rubiginosa,* smells like sweet apples after a rain shower. One of its varieties, 'Lord Penzance', has fleeting flowers in buff tinged with pink. And in the aptly named incense rose, *R. primula,* the fragrance comes mainly from the new shoot growths.

OPPOSITE ABOVE RIGHT

Old-fashioned shrub roses work well with lilies, as well as a froth of herbs such as lavender and lady's mantle around the base, to hide their bare legs.

OPPOSITE BELOW RIGHT

The buds and stems of the fragrant moss rose, R. 'William Lobb', are covered in glandular hairs that release their spicy scent readily. This shrub rose has an open, arching habit and looks best when given a little support.

head in the clouds

Growing fragrant climbers and wall shrubs over a variety of structures, such as garden arches, pergolas, porches and arbours, is a lovely way of bringing scent closer to nose level.

OPPOSITE *A simple wooden tripod made from rustic poles can provide support for a climbing or lax-stemmed shrub rose, adding an old-fashioned, cottagey feel to the border.*

BELOW CENTRE *The annual sweet pea comes in many colours but look out for the old-fashioned mixtures listed in the seed catalogues – these are the best for fragrance. Cut flowers regularly to maintain production.*

Climbers vary enormously in vigour, and unless carefully trained and pruned, some will produce flowers only at the top of the support and that might be too high to enjoy, so be careful that you pick the right plant for the spot you have in mind.

You could grow a combination of fragrant climbers and wall shrubs around a doorway so that every time you walk in and out of the house or garden shed you smell the perfume. Try the deep-pink-flowered *Clematis montana* var. *rubens* 'Tetrarose', which has about half the vigour of the other cultivars and the bonus of bronzy foliage, combined with the pale-pink-flowered *Jasminum* x *stephanense*. A fragrant entranceway is very welcoming for visitors and you can enhance the experience still further using one or two hanging baskets or wall pots fixed at head height. Fill these with scented annuals such as petunias, *Bidens ferulifolia* and white alyssum or ornamental herbs.

It is a good idea to give your chosen climber the support of a porch or roofed trellis archway when used over a doorway, otherwise the long tendrils will keep getting in the way, and after a rain shower the foliage continues to drip. Roses have always been a popular choice for doorways, especially for period buildings and cottages, but be aware that the ground right next to a building can be very dry and poor – not what roses need at all. If you do plant a rose, prepare a wide area by digging in plenty of organic matter and be ready to water the site until the plant is well established. Many climbing roses develop

BELOW *Trained over a pergola, the sumptuous blooms of wisteria hang down at head height allowing you to drink in the delicious perfume.*

BELOW *While young and pliable, the stems of* Laburnum x watereri *'Vossii' can be trained over a pergola.*

bare stems at the base of the plant, but this can easily be remedied by planting an evergreen shrub such as a honey-scented hebe or aromatic rosemary for camouflage.

The walls of a house act like a huge storage heater and walls that receive a lot of sun radiate warmth at night. Plants that would normally be too tender to grow in the open garden are often successful here. These include the climbers *Trachelospermum jasminoides* 'Variegatum' and vanilla-scented *Clematis armandii,* and wall shrubs including the autumn blooming *Camellia sasanqua* 'Narumigata', winter-flowering *Azara microphylla* with its fluffy yellow blooms that smell of vanilla custard, and the refined *Buddleja fallowiana.* The warmth also has the effect of encouraging blooms to release even more perfume – wonderful for sitting out on the patio after sunset or for bedroom fragrance. Imagine drifting off on a sultry summer's evening with wafts of jasmine coming through the open window. Climbers have to be sufficiently vigorous to reach upstairs windows, but given proper support, not only *Jasminum officinale* but also *Clematis montana* cultivars, wisteria and vigorous roses, such as *R.* 'Etoile de Holland, Climbing' or 'Madame Alfred Carrière', will be there in no time. The latter will tolerate some shade but is prone to mildew: if you still want a blush-pink rose but one with excellent health, choose 'New Dawn', which reaches a more modest height of 3m/10ft.

A subtle, but very effective method of attaching climbers and wall shrubs to walls is to use horizontal lines of galvanized training wire threaded through vine eyes and set 45cm/18in apart. Either tap the vine eyes into the mortar or, for screw fittings, drill using a masonry bit and insert a wall plug. With stiff-branched climbers such as roses, you will

BELOW *'Elizabeth', one of the most attractive cultivars of* Clematis montana, *smothers a wall with light bronze foliage and pale pink vanilla-scented blooms.*

need to tie in the shoots as they grow using soft twine. Pull the branches horizontal where possible, to avoid bare stems lower down, and never tuck them behind the wires, or they may get damaged as they grow. For climbers with a twining habit or those that use tendrils, attach a network of vertical wires as well, otherwise the plant will fail to climb on its own.

Another wonderful way to experience the perfume of head-high blooms is to build a pergola over the terrace or along a walkway, using heavy wooden or rough stone pillars for the uprights. Trellis panels used as occasional infills help to create an even greater sense of enclosure as you stroll through the dappled shade, drinking in the fragrance. Any of the more vigorous scented climbers can be used including rambler roses; jasmines; *Clematis montana* varieties such as 'Mayleen', 'Odorata' or the vanilla-scented 'Elizabeth'; as well as vigorous honeysuckles including the white-flowered *Lonicera japonica* 'Halliana'. But one of the most spectacular plants for a pergola is the wisteria, its luxuriant, pendulous blooms in colours ranging from pure white through to deep purple, hanging down beneath the foliage to stunning effect. There are a number of cultivars that are particularly noted for their fragrance, including *Wisteria* 'Burford' (lilac-blue), *W. x formosa* 'Issai' (lilac-blue) and *W* 'Caroline' (deep blue-purple). Always buy named grafted stock or plants grown from cuttings, as seed-raised wisteria can take years to flower. Established plants must be pruned in summer and again in late winter to keep them in bounds and encourage flowering. For a similar effect using yellow blooms, untrained saplings of *Laburnum x watereri* 'Vossii' can be grown up over the pergola framework but the young growths must be tied in regularly while still pliable.

spring essence

The fresh fragrances of early-flowering bulbs banish the tired mood of the last weeks of winter and alert us to the coming of spring and a new growing season.

One of the lovely attributes of spring bulbs is that so many of them produce fragrant flowers. Among the most potent is the hyacinth, the scent of which is almost overpowering indoors. But outside, you do not even need to bend down to smell the flowers. On a sheltered sunny patio, pots of hyacinths will fill the area with perfume. Grape hyacinths, such as *Muscari armeniacum* 'Heavenly Blue', form low carpets of intense blue, honey-scented spikes, ideal for edging a shrub border or pathway since the grassy foliage is persistent. The flower is a favourite of one of the first insects on the scene, the bumble bee.

Early-flowering dwarf bulbs with a delicate fragrance are perfect for planting in window boxes or in pots raised up on a trestle or stepped display unit so that you can smell them more easily. Try the many varieties of *Crocus chrysanthus*; blue-flowered *Iris reticulata* and hybrids such as the deep purple *I.* 'George'; and certain colours of mini cyclamen (particularly red). This winter flowering houseplant, a dwarf form of *Cyclamen persicum*, will thrive in the shelter of an open porch in temperate regions once hardened off. Snowdrops do not enjoy being grown in containers and some kinds, such as *Galanthus elwesii,* are temperamental, favouring free-draining, lime-rich soil. The common snowdrop,

FAR LEFT *The late winter or early spring flowering* Iris reticulata *and forms such as the dark purple* I. *'George' may be grown in pots to bring into the porch where their fragrance can be appreciated.*

BELOW LEFT *Some* Cyclamen persicum *varieties have a lovely perfume and are ideal for pots in a sheltered spot.*

BELOW LEFT *The true blue grape hyacinths are easy to grow and in sufficient quantity their honey-sweet fragrance fills the air.*

BELOW *Grow the little jonquil daffodil 'Quail' in pots raised up off the ground so that you can smell the delicious fragrance more easily.*

Galanthus nivalis, and the double-flowered *G. nivalis* 'Flore Pleno' like moisture-retentive soil rich in organic matter and prefer dappled shade. They are an uplifting sight coming up in drifts beneath trees in early spring. Outside you may not be able to smell the flowers but if a handful of blooms is brought inside, the honey-sweet scent develops.

Certain types of daffodil have a surprisingly strong fragrance and like forced hyacinths, the scent from a bowl full of *Narcissus papyraceus,* more commonly known as 'Paper White', can be almost overpowering indoors. But in the garden the fragrance is enchanting. Dainty jonquils such as *N.* 'Quail' and 'Sweetness', and multi-headed tazzetta types, including 'Geranium' and 'Minnow', need full sun and shelter to thrive, so pots on a patio or a border at the base of a sunny wall would suit. Flowering later are the poeticus or pheasant's eye narcissi, typically with a small dark orange or red 'eye', and these are often fragrant. Water well if the late-spring weather turns dry. On a larger scale altogether, the perfumed, frilly blooms of the double daffodils add a romantic note and include the popular 'Cheerfulness', 'Yellow Cheerfulness' and the creamy yellow 'Winston Churchill'.

BELOW *The sweet perfume of the snowdrop is not usually detected in the open, but pick a posy and bring it into a warm room, and you will be amazed at how it fills the room.*

fleeting fragrance

Some of the most evocative scents of the summer come from quick-flowering annual blooms.
Select old-fashioned varieties to re-create the fragrance of the traditional cottage garden.

ABOVE *Less powerfully scented than the evening blooming* Nicotiana alata, *modern hybrid tobacco plants (* N. x sanderae*) now come in a range of colours with some types sufficiently dwarf and compact to be grown in containers and windowboxes.*

OPPOSITE *The hardy biennial sweet William (* Dianthus barbatus*) is a traditional cottage garden plant with lovely clove-scented blooms.*

The great thing about annuals is that they can be worked into any small space and will quickly fill it with colour and perfume. Fragrant sweet peas (*Lathyrus odoratus*) will scramble up fencing and look lovely growing up wicker or cane wigwams adding height, colour and scent to the border. Hardy annuals such as candytuft (*Iberis odorata*) and poached egg plant (*Limnanthes douglasii*) can be sown where they are to flower. Sweet sultan (*Centaurea moschata*) and the greenish-white-flowered mignonette (*Reseda odorata*) add scent to the mixed border, and despite having quite insignificant purple blooms, the evening fragrance of night-scented stock (*Matthiola bicornis*) is powerful. Sprinkle its seed between other flowers alongside pathways and in beds around the patio or troughs beneath windows. Several nasturtium varieties such as *Tropaeolum* 'Gleam Hybrids' have a delicate perfume, and container-grown plants are useful for slotting into gaps in the border or for hanging baskets.

Summer bedding (half-hardy annuals) can be bought as plants in spring, to be planted out after the last frosts have safely passed. Some of the old-fashioned cottage varieties have an excellent fragrance, but with the exception of petunias, pansies and cherry pie (*Heliotropium* 'Marine'), these are rarely available as plants so you will probably have to raise them from seed. A good example is the flowering tobacco: most modern hybrids (*Nicotiana* x *sanderae*) have very little of the delicious evening scent that characterizes the old seed mixtures of *N. alata*.

Although classed as biennials, the honey-sweet violas and pansies can be grown as half-hardy annuals for summer blooming. Biennials flower in their second year from sowing but once you have them in the garden they will often self-seed. Evening primrose (*Oenothera biennis*), various stocks (forms of *Matthiola bicornis*) and sweet William (*Dianthus barbatus*) are all summer flowering. For late spring blooms grow richly fragrant wallflowers.

BELOW Limnanthes douglasii *(pictured) and sweet white alyssum produce hummocks of honey-scented blooms, ideal for edging and softening paving.*

perfumed perennials

There are so many beautiful summer-blooming perennials that it can be difficult to know which ones to choose from looks alone, but selection is simpler if you pick only those plants with fragrance.

Generally, the closer a plant is to its wild form, the greater the chance of it being scented. Unnatural colours, double or larger-than-usual blooms are features that have often been bred into the plant at the expense of perfume. The daylilies are a case in point: the small yellow-bloomed species, *Hemerocallis citrina, H. dumortieri, H. lilioasphodelus* and *H. middendorfii,* all have a lovely scent, yet few of the cultivars have any scent at all. Exceptions are *H.* 'Hyperion', 'Marion Vaughn' and 'Golden Chimes', all of which have yellow blooms, the latter being very close in appearance to the species.

Whichever perennials you grow, make the most of their fragrance by planting in bold clumps or, if you have room, large swathes. This not only intensifies the perfume, it also makes it easier to detect the different elements and subtleties. Do not plant just one plum tart iris (*Iris graminea*) – plant ten and breathe in the delicious aroma of stewed plums. Or if you prefer a more conventional perfume, such as orange blossom, plant a large stand of pale lavender-coloured *Iris pallida* var. *dalmatica.* This would be beautiful in front of one of the old roses with pink or crimson blooms.

Many of the old-fashioned cottage-garden perennials, such as violets, pinks and the purple-flowered *Iris germanica,* are endowed with scent. They were greatly valued in the days when there were so many unpleasant smells to mask. Dame's violet or sweet rocket (*Hesperis matronalis*) is a typical example. The tall stems bear pink or white single flowers

BELOW *The ancient
lily-of-the-valley is
renowned for its fragrance,
and has long been grown
for cutting. Leave
undisturbed in a cool
spot to form a carpet.*

with a heavy, sweet fragrance that becomes more intense in the evening. It is short-lived and older plants should be discarded in favour of the seedlings that crop up in the vicinity. Another simple flower, the spring-blooming lily-of-the-valley (*Convallaria majalis*), has an exquisite perfume. But this diminutive perennial is not so easy to please, requiring deep moisture-retentive soil with plenty of organic matter to thrive. It looks most at home in a semi-wild area or when growing beneath a small tree. Other wild garden perennials to grow *en masse* include the frothy, cream meadowsweet (*Filipendula ulmaria*), false Solomon's seal (*Smilacina racemosa*), with its cream plumes, and the Himalayan cowslip (*Primula florindae*), all of which like moist ground.

Pinks, carnations and the biennial sweet William belong to the genus *Dianthus* and are classic plants for fragrance. When old-fashioned pinks were crossed with perpetual-flowering carnations, a new breed of plants, the modern pinks, was born. These have larger flowers produced in quantity ranging in colour from white through pinks and purples to ruby red, though there is the odd yellow exception. Some of them, including the salmon-pink *D.* 'Doris', have a lovely sweet, spicy scent and with their evergreen foliage they are ideal for the front of the border. The old-fashioned pinks, such as the white, fringed *D.* 'Mrs Sinkins', flower in early summer and most are richly clove-scented.

As if to break the rules regarding the link with simplicity of bloom and scent, forms of the border peony (*Paeonia lactiflora*) are fragrant almost without exception. This group contains some of the most sumptuous blooms, with single to fully double tissue-paper

BELOW CENTRE
*The exotic-looking
blooms of the hybrid lily
'Star Gazer' fulfil their
promise of heady and
intoxicating perfume
when they flower in late
summer. Unlike many
lilies, this one is relatively
compact and needs
little support.*

flowers that often have incredibly intricate centres. *P. l.* 'Duchesse de Nemours' is a confection of pale green, white and creamy yellow, while the double-flowered 'Félix Crousse' (syn. 'Victor Hugo') is a rich carmine with a dark centre. Certain lilies have the same air of luxury. For large, heavily scented trumpets choose the pure white *Lilium regale*, or forms from the soft orange African Queen Group or fuchsia-pink Pink Perfection Group. Somewhat shorter, though just as exotic, is *L.* 'Star Gazer', which has star-shaped carmine blooms with deeper spotting.

Two other fragrant bulbs for the mixed border include the elegant midsummer flowering Cape hyacinth (*Galtonia candicans*) with drooping white, waxy bells and *Gladiolus callianthus* (formerly *Acidanthera*), which flowers from late summer to early autumn and has white blooms with a prominent maroon blotch. Like the lilies, these look attractive rising up above surrounding herbaceous plants.

Tender perennials, bulbs and tubers extend the scope for fragrant flowers further. If the roots are protected with a deep mulch, or if the plants are grown at the foot of a wall, some, such as crinum lilies and *Amaryllis belladonna*, may survive the winter outdoors. The tall verbena (*Verbena bonariensis*) is a wonderful sight when it seeds right through a border sending up a 1.8m/6ft high forest of thin, wiry stems each topped with clusters of lavender flowers. In containers or for ground cover in borders, try the yellow-flowered *Bidens ferulifolia* with its profusion of honey-scented yellow blooms, and seek out old cultivars grown from cuttings like *Heliotropium arborescens* 'Chatsworth' and 'Gatton Park'.

ABOVE *The ruffled, tissue-paper blooms of border peonies are often beautifully fragrant. These long-lived perennials, flowering in the early part of summer, also have attractive spring foliage.*

cool fragrances

A surprising number of shrubs that bloom from autumn to spring are scented. It is wonderful to detect a beautiful fragrance at a time when there are few flowers about – and their perfumes are heavenly.

BELOW *The aptly named* Daphne odora *blooms from midwinter to early spring, forming tight flower clusters at the ends of its twiggy stems. Grow this evergreen in a sheltered corner.*

Shrubs that flower in the winter months often have a powerful scent, completely out of proportion with the size of their flowers. This is likely to be because pollinating insects are so few and far between and the plants need a far-reaching, non-visual signal to attract them. A typical example is the low evergreen *Sarcococca*, whose insignificant white blooms are potently fragrant. Although their scent is so welcome in the winter months, when summer comes many of the winter-flowering shrubs look rather dull, so species like the shrubby honeysuckle (*Lonicera fragrantissima*), witch hazels such as *Hamamellis* x *intermedia* 'Pallida' and winter sweet (*Chimonanthus praecox*) are best used as background plantings. Daphnes are well known for their fragrant blooms and *Daphne bholua* 'Jacqueline Postill' and *D. b.* 'Gurkha' are two relative newcomers to look out for. A more familiar winter-flowering species is the mezereon, *D. mezereum*, with fragrant deep-pink blooms smothering the bare stems in late winter.

A sheltered position is always desirable for winter blooms so that the scent is not dissipated by wind, and a warm wall would be perfect for a Japanese apricot. *Prunus mume* 'Beni-chidori,' with deep-pink flowers, and the double white flowered 'Omoi-no-mama' are both highly fragrant and, unusually for this time of year, ornamental. When in full bloom, the winter-flowering *Viburnum* x *bodnantense* 'Dawn' also puts on quite a show with its rich pink pompom flowers of almond sweetness. The drooping yellow flower clusters of *Mahonia japonica* (smelling like lily-of-the-valley) and the upright spikes of *Mahonia* x *media* cultivars such as 'Charity' and 'Winter Sun' deserve centre stage.

Many spring-flowering shrubs are noted for the way they scent the air, including the exotic-looking *Rhododendron luteum*, a yellow-blooming woodland azalea requiring acid, moisture-retentive soil and light shade. The male and female forms of *Skimmia* are generally more lime tolerant. The flower buds of male plants such as *Skimmia* x *confusa* 'Kew Green' and *S. japonica* 'Rubella' are an ornamental feature throughout the winter, and their perfume is a bonus in spring. Despite having only tiny white flowers, *Osmanthus* x *burkwoodii* and the later flowering *O. delavayi* are both fragrant and the large pink-tinged domed heads of *Viburnum* x *carlcephalum* smell exactly like carnations.

ABOVE *In early autumn, the tiny white blooms of* Elaeagnus x ebbingei, *which are virtually hidden by the foliage, release a sweet, spicy aroma that can be detected some distance from the plant, baffling passers-by.*

OPPOSITE *In late spring and early summer, varieties of the common lilac (*Syringa vulgaris*) open their fragrant blooms.*

a scented herb garden

If you go to a specialist herb nursery you will find a huge range of plants that were once grown for their health-giving properties. Some are now historical curiosities, but all have interesting fragrances to enjoy.

Herbs were once the mainstay of medical practitioners, and many were also used for a bewildering array of household purposes. When you rub their foliage to release the aromatic oils, you will find you like some smells and find others strange, though not necessarily unpleasant. Pick what appeals even if the aromas seem a little odd – if you like them they may well do you good. Eau de Cologne mint (*Mentha x piperita* f. *citrata*) and lemon balm (*Melissa officinalis*) have stems of fresh-smelling leaves that are wonderful for cutting for the house, and some sweet herbs such as bergamot (*Monarda*) and scented-leaf geraniums (*Pelargonium*) are ingredients of pot pourris.

Sometimes, when there is a herb scent that you just do not seem to be able to get enough of, the reason is because it forms a memory link to a particular time or place. Any plant whose pleasing aroma makes you want to smell it over and over should be grown in abundance. This could include any of the culinary herbs, such as bay, sweet basil, thyme, rosemary, sage, fennel, hyssop, tarragon, marjoram and mint. You may also want to incorporate plants that have a long tradition of being grown in herb gardens, including the evergreen lavenders, cotton lavender (*Santolina chamaecyparissus*) and wormwoods (*Artemisia*) as well as chamomile and catmint (*Nepeta x faassenii*). The latter herb is a powerful cat aphrodisiac and they just love to roll around and luxuriate in its foliage.

BELOW *Many of the traditional and less well-known herbs are decorative and can easily be worked in with other border flowers.*

Recently, catmint has also been shown to contain a chemical that is one of the most effective mosquito repellents. Perhaps this would be a good plant to surround a patio used for evening entertaining.

Apart from traditional herbs, there are many other shrubs, trees and perennials with aromatic foliage and there is no reason why these could not be mixed into a herb garden. Take the dainty, minty-smelling calamints, including forms of *Calamintha nepeta,* which have tiny white, lilac or mauve flowers attractive to butterflies and bees. The low hummocks bloom from midsummer into autumn. A relatively recent arrival, and another plant for the front of the border, is the domed Australian mint bush, *Prostanthera cuneata,* whose dark green, rounded and slightly glossy leaves have a peppermint aroma. Though small, the pale lilac summer flowers make quite a feature. The tall, airy, blue spires of Russian sage (*Perovskia atriplicifolia*) make a late show in the garden, and after the flowers have faded, the silvery stems remain ornamental, lasting well into winter. The finely cut leaves have a sinus-clearing pungency. Another late-flowering aromatic shrub is *Caryopteris* x *clandonensis,* which has pleasantly aromatic foliage. Choose from a range of named cultivars, all with varying shades of blue flowers, for example, 'Heavenly Blue' and 'Ferndown'. Perovskia and caryopteris both work well combined with silver- and grey-leaved herbs.

Myrtle (*Myrtus communis*) is a plant that has a long history of garden cultivation. It is rather tender but can survive outdoors in a sheltered spot in mild areas. The small, glossy, dark evergreen leaves are sweetly aromatic when crushed, and from

BELOW LEFT *There are many carpeting and hummock forming thymes to choose from. All enjoy sharp drainage and work well in and around paved areas where the aroma is released underfoot.*

BELOW *The tufted French lavender (Lavandula stoechas), of which there are now several excellent varieties, flowers over a long period and as well as being aromatic is highly ornamental.*

BELOW RIGHT *Purple
and plain green forms
of the common sage
(*Salvia officinalis*)
make low evergreen
hummocks, ideal for
border edging. You could
use cotton lavender
(*Santolina*), hyssop,
catmint or lavender to
similar effect.*

mid- to late summer a profusion of fluffy white flowers open from spherical buds. If you have somewhere to overwinter plants, myrtle makes a neat, attractive bush for pots on the patio. Eucalyptus has a powerful scent and it is fun to have some growing in the garden. Left unpruned, this Australasian plant quickly makes a tall, slender evergreen tree. With annual pruning, however, the blue-grey-leaved *Eucalyptus gunnii* can be kept as a bush with rounded juvenile foliage, lovely for cutting. Another aromatic sensation is the evergreen conifer *Thuja plicata*. Commonly used for hedging, the foliage smells of peardrop candy when clipped or after a rainstorm.

A pleasant job in the garden is to clip over the lavender bushes and hedges with a pair of shears once the flower stems have faded. This promotes bushy growth and the aroma released during clipping is extremely rewarding. Working in a herb garden with a wide spectrum of aromatic plants is pleasurable because every disturbance creates a fresh smell for you to inhale and appreciate. To make the most of aromas and perfumes, create shelter using tall hedges or fences as well as overhead structures to trap the volatile oils and prevent them from dissipating. Provided it does not create too much shade over the sun-loving herbs, a pergola walkway with a light canopy of climbers could be added. A situation in full sun with plenty of paving will help to generate the heat required to make the plants release their aromatic oils. A pool and fountain will increase the intensity of the fragrance by keeping the atmosphere moist. Do not forget to include seating so that you can relax in this special, scented place and benefit from the therapeutic effects of all those delicious fragrances.

surprising scents

We are intrigued and excited when a plant reminds us of something completely different –
the experience is one of the best surprises in the garden.

BELOW *The scent*
emanating from the
aptly named chocolate
cosmos seems a perfect
match for the rich
dark blooms of this
tender perennial.

Who would have thought that sage could smell of blackcurrants, but *Salvia microphylla* var. *microphylla* has this aroma. It may also come as a surprise to learn that when you crush the multicoloured leaves of *Houttuynia cordata* 'Chameleon' they smell just like Seville oranges, and the silver-leaved shrub *Helichrysum italicum* smells of curry.

Chocoholics will be delighted to learn that several plants release a chocolate aroma, either from the flowers or foliage – gathering up fallen walnut tree leaves in autumn has this unexpected bonus. Chocolate scent wafts from the flowers of the vigorous

OPPOSITE *Though*
not usually noted as an
aromatic plant, the
colourful leaves of
Houttuynia cordata
'Chameleon' release a
scent reminiscent of
Seville oranges.

climber *Clematis montana* var. *wilsonii* (white with yellow stamens), from the dark maroon-flowered tender perennial, chocolate cosmos (*Cosmos atrosanguineus*), and the small blooms of the shrubs *Corokia* x *virgata* and *Pittosporum tenuifolium*. Still on sweet things, if you detect the delicious smell of caramelizing sugar on a fine autumn day, it may well be coming from the leaves of *Cercidophyllum japonicum*. As a genus, the sun roses (*Cistus*) exude a sweet, sticky aromatic gum, which is volatile when hot, scenting the air. *Cistus ladanifer* is particularly strong.

In summer try smelling the yellow pea flowers of the appropriately named pineapple broom, *Cytisus battanderi,* or rubbing the leaves of the pineapple sage (*Salvia elegans* 'Scarlet Pineapple'), which has spikes of red blooms. The yellow ball-shaped flower clusters of Jerusalem sage (*Phlomis fruticosa*) smell rather like fruity bubble gum, and after a rain shower the foliage of the eglantine

rose (*Rosa rubiginosa*) smells like apples. And the crushed leaves of the winter-flowering *Viburnum* x *bodnantense* 'Dawn' remind you of sweet green (bell) peppers.

The scented-leaf pelargoniums smell of a whole range of different things. Some are distinctly medicinal, reminding you of wintergreen or camphor for example; while others smell like attar of roses, oranges, apples and various mints. The lemon-scented *Pelargonium crispum* and *P. citriodorum* only have to be lightly brushed to release a cloud of tangy aroma – wonderful in pots for the summer patio. If you have a warm sheltered wall, you could grow one of the most potent citrus-smelling shrubs of all, the lemon verbena (*Aloysia triphylla*). Another strongly aromatic plant is lemon balm (*Melissa officinalis*), which also has attractive yellow-variegated and gold leaf forms. This relative of the mint is useful in a wild, shady corner of the garden or for growing in a large clump next to a gate. The smell is just like lemon sherbet. To combat mildew and replace tired foliage mid-season, cut to the ground and feed and water well to promote regrowth. The lemon-scented thyme (*Thymus* x *citriodorus*) is great for cracks in paving and as a foreground filler for scented window boxes. Other flowers that smell of lemons include the big waxy blooms of *Magnolia grandiflora* and the white blooms of the rose 'Margaret Merril'.

Index of common plant names

Page numbers in italics refer to photograph captions.

General index

acknowledgements

The publishers would like to thank the following sculptors, garden designers and garden owners for permission to use their work:

t top, c centre, b bottom, l left, r right

Peter Anderson (photographer), p5c, p5r, p20b, p21, p48r, p17r, p35tr, p47bl, p48r, p49, p53, p62, p63r, p65l, p88, p101l, p101r, p104b, p104l, p110l, p111l, p112, p113b, p114l, p115l, p116b, p118bl, p118br, p 120r, p126l, p126b, p128l, p129l, p130b, p130t, p133r, p135tl, p135bl, p137r, p138b, p139, p140bl, p144l, p146b, p147b, p147t, p148t, p156. The following images were taken at Edmondsham House, Edmondsham, Wimborne, Dorset, UK. Open to the public April to October. p1, p8, p12, p56. The following images were taken at the Centre For Alternative Technology, Machynlleth, Powys, Wales, UK: p52l, p74r, p87. The following images were taken at Audley End Organic Kitchen Garden: p51l and p57. The following images were taken at the Henry Doubleday Research Association (HDRA), Ryton Organic Gardens, Coventry, UK: p73r, p77, p81b, p83, p85.

Norio Asai (photographer), p18b.

Martin Brigdale (photographer), p40.

Jonathan Buckley (photographer), p15, p16l, p19, p30l, p30r, p31, p36r, p42t, p42b, p43, p58l, p59, p72l, p72r, p74l, p75, p76l, p76r, p78l, p78r, p79, p80t, p81t, p82l, p82r, p84l, p84r, p86b, p86r, p89l, p89c, p89r, p95l, p102t, p115r, p118tl, p129r, p137b, p140l, p141l, p141r, p142, p143t, p143b, p145, p146l, p148b, p153l, p157, p158, p159, p160.

Sarah Cuttle (photographer), p2, p3, p61t, p64l.

Polly Eltes (photographer), p54l mosaic by Sheryl Wilson of Reptile, p64r mosaic by Rebecca Newnham.

John Freeman (photographer), p136.

Michelle Garrett (photographer), p35tl, p36l, p91r, p94l, p96, p97 all, p98l, p98b, p116t.

Christine Hanscomb (photographer), p4.

Marie O'Hara (photographer), p14, p32l, p34, p35br, p45b, p45r, p66l, p67, p68l, p71tl, p102b, p133b, p135tr.

Jacqui Hurst (photographer), p22t.

Andrea Jones (photographer), p11, p24r, p47br, p73l, p90, p92, p93b, p93r, p94c, p95c, p95r, p111r, p113r, p151r, p152l, p152b, p153r.

Simon McBride (photographer), p17l, p18l, p26, p27b, p100l, p114c, p118tr, p120l, p140br.

James Mitchell (photographer), endpaper.

Debbie Patterson (photographer), p10, p20l, p23b, p23r, p24l, p27r, p28t, p32b, p41tl, p41tr, p41b, p44, p46, p47t, p48l, p71b, p100r, p125, p138l.

Spike Powell (photographer), p71tr.

Juliette Wade (photographer), p25br.

Jo Whitworth (photographer), p9 (in the garden of Judy Wiseman, N. Finchley, London, UK), p16r, p25t and p39 (sculpture by Ivan Hicks, "The Garden in Mind", Stanstead, Rowlands, Castle, Hampshire, UK), p22b (garden design by Marylynn Abbott at West Green House Garden, near Hartney, Wintney, Hampshire, UK), p25bl (at Iford Manor, Bradford-on-Avon, Wiltshire, UK), p28b (at The Old Vicarage, East Rushton, Norfolk, UK), p29 (sculpture by Petu Randall-Page at The New Art Centre Sculpture Park & Gallery, Roche Court, near Salisbury, Wiltshire, UK), p33b, p35bl, p52b (garden design by Gay Wilson), p51r and p60 (at Julia van den Bosch's garden, Ham, London), p55br, p65r ("Sculpture in the Garden" designed by George Carter and photographed at the RHS Chelsea Flower Show, 1999), p66r, p70 (at Hillbarn House, Great Bedwyn, Wiltshire, UK), p108,

p109b, p109r ("Horti-Couture" designed by James Alexander-Sinclair at the Chelsea Flower Show, 1999), p123b, p123r, p127r. The following images were taken at The Hannah Peschar Sculpture Garden, Black and White Cottage, Ockley, Surrey, UK (designed by Anthony Paul, landscape designer): p63b, p107 (pictish spiral bench in green oak by Nigel Ross), p110r, p122 (bridge designed by Anthony Paul).

Peter Williams (photographer), p55bl.

Polly Wreford (photographer), p99.

The publishers wold like to thank the following for permission to reproduce their images:

Jenny Hendy: p5l, p6, p13, p24c (The Lance Hattatt Design Garden, Herefordshire, UK), p33t, p37, p58r, p103 Allison Armour-Wilson's aqualens at the RHS Chelsea Flower Show, 2000), p105, p106, p117, p124l (mosaic by Maggy Howarth for Arabella Lennox-Boyd), p135br, (in the garden of Alice Palser), p144b at Dorothy Clive Gardens, p150, p151b.
The Bruce Coleman Collection: p50l photo by Kim Taylor, p55t by Robert Maier.
The Garden Picture Library: p50r and p69 photo by Marijke Heuff, p61b photo by Amanda Knapp, p68b and p132 photos by Steven Wooster, p80b and p155 photos by JS Sira, p121 photo by Kit Young, p127l, photo by Janet Sorrell, p131 photo by Marie O'Hara, p149 photo by Mayer, p154 photo by David Cavagnaro.

Jacket front and spine by Peter Anderson, front flap and "scent" picture on back by Andrea Jones, back: "sight", "sound" and "touch" by Jonathan Buckley, "taste" by Debbie Patterson.